Yoga in Action
Karma Yoga

Brahmrishi Vishvatma Bawra
Lectures on
The *Bhagavad Gītā* and *Karma Yoga*

Compiled and Edited by
William F. & Margot S. Milcetich
Yogendra & Devhuti

Brahmrishi Yoga Publications

Publisher: Brahmrishi Yoga Publications
BrahmrishiYoga.org

Date: May 2010

© Brahmrishi Yoga Publications

All rights reserved

No part of this book may be used or reproduced in any manner without written permission, except in the case of brief quotations embodied in critical articles and reviews.

Printed in United States of America

Library of Congress Control Number: 2010905464

ISBN: 978-1-4528-1656-2

Dedicated to Swami Divya Bharti whose quiet and constant care of Swami Bawra's ashram has supported many disciples.

Special thanks to Julie Tamarkin, whose mastery of written English and love of philosophy enhance the clarity of Swami Bawra's thought.

Contents

Preface i
Introduction... 1

Philosophy of *Karma Yoga*

    Verses 1 & 2 13
    Verse 3 21
    Verse 4.. 30
    Verses 5-7 35
    Verse 8.. 42

Foundation of *Karma Yoga*

    Verses 9 & 10...................................... 47
    Verse 11.. 54
    Verses 12 & 13 62
    Verses 14 & 15 70

Putting *Karma Yoga* into Practice

    Self-Cultivation.................................... 76
    Practical Knowledge 83
    Devotion... 87
    The Enemy is Desire 93
    Love Seeks its Source......................... 98
    Yagya... 103

Preface

Brahmrishi Vishvatma Bawra (1934-2002) is the founder of the International Brahmrishi Mission. Swami Bawra's teaching emphasizes that the spiritual science of *Brahma Vidya*, knowledge of the source of life, has two aspects: theory and practice. In the *Upanishads* and *Bhagavad Gītā* the theory of this science is called *Sāmkhya*, and its practical aspect is *Yoga*. On the basis of his own experiences, Swami Bawra taught us to realize ultimate truth in order to find freedom from suffering. His teachings are universal and not related with any creed, color, country, community, gender, or sect.

This book is inspired by three series of lectures on the *Bhagavad Gītā* Swami Bawra gave in Kent, Ohio, in 1995, 1997 and 1998. The 1998 lectures are a commentary on the first fifteen verses of the third chapter of the *Bhagavad Gītā*, highlighting the philosophy and foundation of *karma yoga*. The 1997 lectures were originally compiled in *Essays on Karma Yoga*. The introduction and the topics in "Putting Karma Yoga into Practice" are based on these general discussions about *karma yoga*. The final chapter, "*Yagya*," is derived from the 1995 lectures on the fourth chapter of the *Bhagavad Gītā*, previously compiled in *The Nature of Sacrifice*.

To assist the English reader with the pronunciation of frequently used Sanskrit terms, letters have been added to the strict transliteration of Sanskrit to English. For example, *citta* is written as *chitta*. Additionally, the long vowels of a, i, and u are indicated by the symbols, ā, ī, and

i

ū. There is no capitalization in Sanskrit, so the use of capitalization is always a deliberate choice. As systems of philosophy, *Sāmkhya*, *Vedanta* and *Yoga* are capitalized. When the terms *sāmkhya* and *yoga* refer to methods of practice, these terms are not capitalized. *Brahman*, God, Godhead and Lord are capitalized. Traditionally, the pronoun for formless *Brahman* is "That," and formful *Brahman* is "He." Within the *Bhagavad Gītā*, Krishna is considered an incarnation of Godhead, and use of the pronoun "He" refers to Krishna as God and as *Brahman*.

Introduction

The *Vedas* are an ancient compilation of universal truth and wisdom. The knowledge in the *Vedas* focuses on four subject areas, which correspond to four aspects of human life. The first three are related with the head, heart, and hands. Head indicates wisdom, heart represents love, and hands refer to action. The fourth focus is absolute truth, the supreme source of all.

A primary philosophical question is: Why do humans suffer? The *Vedas* answer: We suffer because we believe we will find happiness in worldly pleasures. We think our happiness depends on transitory situations, people and things. Every circumstance, relationship and possession is temporary. Everything found in human life has a beginning and an end. When these transitory means do not meet our expectations or, worse, when they satisfy us for a while but then change or cease to be, we suffer. The *Vedas* offer a scientific method to free us from our suffering and lead us toward lasting bliss. The teachings on absolute truth point us toward eternal happiness. Absolute truth is the source of life. Many names have been given to this source, but it remains one, absolute, infinite truth. If we are not aware of this supreme source then we use our head, heart, and hands to pursue transitory objects. But if we are aware of this unchanging, absolute level of existence, and we learn how to act in the world while aiming toward oneness with truth, then we move toward eternal happiness and peace.

Most often, we direct our wisdom, love, and action toward worldly objects, without thinking of absolute truth. When we do this, our love is associated with people and objects; it is temporary and cycles in and out of existence. When a person or object no longer satisfies us, we suffer because our love is lost, and we desire a replacement. This cycle of desire, action, attainment, and loss is endless.

We act in every moment of life, but we are often unaware of what motivates our actions and we do not understand the consequences of our behavior. Our actions can drag us toward suffering or lift us toward supreme truth. Action or movement is inherent in nature and we cannot live a single moment without it. Our lives are made up of a series of actions: we breathe, we talk, we think, we sleep, we move. Even the decision to resist action is an action. Our choice is whether to act in order to feed the body and senses in a cycle of desire and loss, or to strive toward the highest good of eternal peace and happiness. We have all the means for action: intellect, ego, mind, senses, and body. Nature bestows these tools, which are necessary for experiencing the world and for achieving infinite wisdom and bliss. How we use these instruments depends on our understanding of reality, our motivation for action and our effort. When we are ignorant of truth and our actions are motivated by the external environment, we experience excitement and frustration, desire and fear, temporary pleasure and ultimate suffering in a cycle that spirals downward. But when our actions are inspired by an inner demand for infinite wisdom, we uplift ourselves toward eternal peace. The science of action presented in the *Vedas* teaches us how to use our human abilities to gain absolute truth.

When we disregard the divine aim of life and remain busy with worldly affairs, we waste the span of life bestowed by divinity. Life is not for accumulation, but for realizing our supreme source. We must understand the goal of life and the means for attaining this aim, and use all of our means to achieve the highest good. We can transform our humanity into divinity through thought, love, and action.

No transformation comes by isolating and developing only one aspect of ourselves: our thinking, emotions, or behavior. Practice includes head, heart and hands, and we use all three to reach toward the supreme source. Knowledge is powerless without application. Love without wisdom is passion or lust. And action without love and wisdom is meaningless. We are humans because of all three, head, heart and hands; all combine on one path to ultimate truth. This path of practice is called *karma yoga*.

When our intellect and heart are filled with divine knowledge and love, then our actions change from the pursuit of worldly objects to the search for divinity. *Yoga* is realizing union with the supreme source, which unites us all. We cannot in any moment be separate from our divine source of life, but we disconnect from our awareness of this truth.

In my tradition, ultimate truth is known as *Brahman*. It is beyond description, but indicated as truth, knowledge, and infinity.[1] Truth and knowledge are both infinite and whatever is infinite cannot be divided. This ultimate truth is the source of our life. Our soul has the same qualities of this source of life. It is infinite and unlimited.

---

[1] *Taittirīya Upanishad* II.1.2.

Just as space cannot be limited by the walls we construct, our soul is not confined by the physical body, nor separated by our mental definitions of self. We think that the space inside of our house is the same at all times, but science tells us the earth orbits around the sun and rotates on an axis. The space within our house is constantly changed by the movements of our earth. We think the space is our space, but in reality we share it in many unknown ways. Likewise, our real self is not divided or limited by this body. We all share one divine source residing within each of us as the conscious supreme self.

Consciousness is not divisible. Supreme consciousness manifests in each entity through a medium that has the capacity to receive the light of consciousness. This medium is given many different names. In the *Upanishads* the medium is called the *brahma chakra*, *Sāmkhya* uses the term intellect, and *Yoga* calls this *chitta*. These terms indicate the same medium that adopts and manifests consciousness. This medium is the first projection of nature or energy and has an individual quality. It is because of this medium that our sense of existence or soul seems contained, just as walls seem to limit space. When this medium is enlivened with consciousness, it is called individual soul because of the individual quality of the medium, not because of any limitation of the soul.

Nowadays, we have the example of a computer chip. A very small chip, made from a tiny piece of silicon, is able to receive and process a vast number of instructions. Our *chitta* is even smaller than a computer chip, yet adopts and manifests infinity in the form of our self. The *chitta* collects and hold millions of impressions from our previous lives. These impressions are the cause of our current physical form, our abilities, and evolutionary development. They determine the span of our lives and structure the results we receive from previous actions or *karma*.

Our abilities and the stage of our evolutionary development include all impressions related with our previous effort toward attaining ultimate truth. Our actions in previous lives are the cause of our situation in this life, and our current actions will shape our next life. In each lifetime, our upliftment or downfall is based on our actions.[2] A teacher provides guidance, but ultimately we must put the teachings into practice. How we receive, process, preserve, use and realize knowledge depends upon our determination. Everything we think and do forms impressions in our *chitta* that structure our personality and become the basis of our future actions and our future situation. We should use our willpower and allow wisdom to guide our actions, integrating wisdom in our head, heart, and hands to attain our goal.

The *Yoga* system considers the body to be composed of three bodies: causal, subtle, and gross. In terms of head, heart and hands, the causal body is related with the head, the subtle body with the heart, and the gross body with the hands. Head indicates the intellect, heart is related with our mind and emotions, and hands represent the senses and the physical body. The causal, subtle and gross bodies are formed by nature or energy, whereas our soul or real self is above these three bodies and is a manifestation of consciousness. Action is related with the body, senses, mind, and intellect, but none of these instruments perform without the presence of the soul. Nature moves only when

---

[2] *Bhagavad Gītā* VI/5.

inspired by spirit. Our physical form and thus all of our actions are made possible because the indwelling spirit is present, and our actions lift us toward infinite wisdom and bliss or take us down into the cycle of desire and disappointment. For this reason the embodied soul or indweller is considered to be the cause for our experience of pleasure and pain.[3]

Our soul is the master of our instruments. Sentience and awareness are the properties of spirit, not nature. Therefore our conscious soul is responsible for our actions. Our soul knows right from wrong; which actions will lift us toward divinity and which behaviors pull us into the maze of desire, fear and anger. It is hard for most of us to hear the guiding wisdom of the soul because the chatter in our mind is so loud. The waves of thought that make up the mind are created by the tidal pull of our impressions. These impressions have been worn into our intellect through the soul's experience of worldly affairs over many lifetimes. Because of these impressions, we have fixed opinions about how things should be, who we are, what is good and what is bad. These patterns of thinking trigger our actions. Our thinking and our behavior are conditioned by our impressions.

In the gross world, we prepare our bodies for athletics by conditioning; we practice physical drills over and over again until our bodies automatically perform with strength and agility. In the same way, we can change the condition of our intellect by committing to practices which help us develop our conscious awareness. Because the actions we perform with the body and senses are driven by the

---

[3] *Bhagavad Gītā* XIII/21.

motives in our mind, developing our conscious awareness leads to meaningful changes in the way we act. When we allow wisdom to guide our actions, we begin to remove unhelpful habits of thinking and doing, replacing them with healthier ones. Healthy impressions generate helpful actions. These teachings on the science of action help us to avoid the harm caused by negative behaviors and live awarefully in the light of divine consciousness.

Our body, senses, mind, and intellect change in every moment. They are projections of energy, always fluctuating. Change is the property of nature. These transitory instruments cannot provide eternal happiness. Therefore, we should not expect eternal peace and happiness when we are engrossed with our faculties in the physical world. Yet these same tools can help us attain the highest good. When we use our abilities to move toward divinity, we continue to act in the world, but we are not attached to the results of our actions. When our behavior is no longer driven by a desire for worldly pleasures or the fear of worldly pain, we achieve lasting peace and happiness.

This is the path of *karma yoga*. In the *Bhagavad Gītā*, Krishna tells Arjuna, "For those practitioners who are eager to attain the highest truth, action is the means. And for those practitioners who have attained the highest truth, tranquility is the means."[4] We must act to gain the highest truth. We use our transitory instruments to realize eternal truth. We begin where we are and gradually move toward a spiritual state. This is called practice. Patanjali explains,

---

[4] *Bhagavad Gītā* VI/3.

"Continuous practice with devotion for a long period of time will bring stability."[5]

We should not think that after one day of seeking guidance from our wisdom, our habits will change. It takes practice. The impressions of experience that cause our current behavior took time to develop, and only in time will we shift toward realization of the highest good. We have spent many lives on this path. With effort and firm faith developed through many lives, *yogis* gradually accomplish their goal.

Krishna tells us, "No effort is ever lost. Even a little of this discipline will free one from great fear."[6] Our intention to move toward divinity will lead us to divinity. When we leave this body, we achieve a divine state and when we return in human form we will start our journey from where we left off. This practice gradually brings peace; our effort toward the goal brings satisfaction.

When we strive for divinity we gain and preserve divine energy. Pursuit of enjoyment scatters our energy. When we engage in physical, mental, sensual, or sexual enjoyment we squander our energy. But when we engage in *yoga* practices, including meditation, a focus on divinity, and the control of our senses, we increase our energy and gain happiness. Our efforts give us peace, and happiness is the result of peace. When we use our energy wisely we find the happiness we seek.

We are responsible for our actions and their results. Our previous actions have brought us to our current position. What has gone before is unfathomable; there are countless previous unknown actions. If we are currently in

---

[5] *Yoga Sūtras* I/17.
[6] *Bhagavad Gītā* II/40.

a challenging or discouraging situation, we should not be afraid. Once the *karma* gives its results, it will be finished. We need to be aware in the present moment and avoid repeating the same mistakes that brought us our current suffering. Otherwise, our future will be just as difficult as our present life.

There are two ways to burn off *karma*. Either we experience the results, good or bad, or we discipline ourselves. When we experience the pleasure or pain resulting from our past actions, our reactions generate more *karma* that binds us in the cycle of pleasure and pain. When we perform penance or austerity, working to control the mind and senses and eliminate desire and temptation, we burn the seeds of *karma*. We gradually detach from the belief that people, objects or the results of our actions will provide us with peace and happiness. We turn inward to realize that our individual existence is one with the source of life, and we root ourselves in eternal peace and happiness. In this way we eliminate the ignorance binding us to the cycle of transitory existence, and we gain an eternal state of emancipation.

Krishna explains that there are two primary paths of *yoga* for attaining emancipation: the path of knowledge and the path of devotion,[7] *sāmkhya yoga* and *karma yoga*.[8] On the battlefield, Krishna teaches Arjuna about both paths, but directs him to follow the path of *karma yoga*. The setting highlights that every soul enters a battlefield where evil is fought and eternal good is preserved. Krishna tells Arjuna, "I am not teaching this knowledge only to you, but for all

---

[7] *Bhagavad Gītā* III/3.
[8] *Sāmkhya* was established by Kapil and *Yoga* by Hiranyagarbha.

humans. Those who follow my divine knowledge will be free from bondage."[9]

Krishna does not deny the path of renunciation and analysis as he encourages the path of action. He begins his teaching with *Sāmkhya*. But he teaches that wisdom has two aspects: wisdom with detachment and wisdom with love. Wisdom with detachment is called the path of knowledge and wisdom with love is called the path of devotion. Wisdom is necessary for both paths.[10]

The path of wisdom with love, *karma yoga*, teaches that all of creation is a manifestation of the supreme Lord. Nature is divine power and has no separate existence or movement without spirit, which is divine light and will. Everything that has a name and takes form is an expression of the supreme cause and is inseparably connected with the divine. We are taught to love all, because all beings are manifestations of the divine. The practitioner of *karma yoga* devotes all instruments, abilities, and strength to the service of all beings, because all beings are manifest forms of one supreme source.

We all share the same source of life, and we receive our life energy from this source. Although the supreme source is beyond our vision and perception, we can realize that it exists and we can approach it. The supreme cause enlightens our *brahma chakra* with divine light and manifests as our life energy or *prāna*. This life energy is called soul and appears in our heart[11] as love.

---

[9] *Bhagavad Gītā* III/31.
[10] *Bhagavad Gītā* II/39.
[11] Philosophically, heart does not mean the physical heart. In Sanskrit, this place is indicated by the word *hridhayam*. It is the

Love is eternal, but when love becomes attached to worldly objects it loses its purity and becomes desire. When love is attached to sexuality, it expresses as passion or lust. With any hindrance, it appears as anger. All emotions are variations of this love. But love is not for worldly objects; it is for devotion. When our love is inspired by devotion, it becomes pure and unselfish and is more nourishing and helpful to the people in our lives.

We can devote our love to any form of divinity. In the beginning there is no need to fix our mind on the supreme Lord. It is difficult to focus on something that is unknown to us. We can begin by making our mind one-pointed on whatever is dear to us, as Patanjali advises.[12] This practice purifies the mind. He also suggests focusing the mind on a person who is perfectly detached.[13] There is one valuable and intimate focus of the mind we all share: our breath. Breath is life.

When we relate our mind with breath, then thought and breath together lead us to our source. Each and every being receives life energy from this supreme source in the form of breath. As we realize our unity with this divine source, we experience divine love, and divine love compels us to serve the divinity manifesting in all beings. Pure love is desireless, and desireless love motivates non-binding actions.

The practitioner of *karma yoga* acts without bondage because all actions are for divinity.[14] The work of the

---

center that initiates the receiving and discharging of breath and is the medium that receives the light of consciousness.

[12] *Yoga Sūtras* I/35.
[13] *Yoga Sūtras* I/37.
[14] *Bhagavad Gītā* V/2.

body, thoughts and speech are related with divine power. The *karma yogi* willingly dedicates all actions to divinity and benefits all beings. Practicing in this way, our entire being is aligned with divinity in every moment. Krishna tells, "Both renunciation with knowledge and the *yoga* of action lead to incomparable bliss. The path of *karma yoga* is superior."[15]

All that we use is a gift of divinity. All that we do is for divinity. All that we see belongs to divinity. Divinity is the root of everything. We are only the medium for divinity to engage with this manifestation. All that exists comes from one supreme cause, exists to serve the supreme cause, and returns to the supreme cause. On this path, we realize divine unity in diversity and we gain emancipation.

---

[15] *Bhagavad Gītā* V/2.

Philosophy of *Karma Yoga*
August 25, 1998

III/1 O my Lord, if in your opinion wisdom is greater than action, why are you urging and guiding me to engage in this dreadful activity?

III/2 Your teaching is creating confusion in my mind. Therefore, tell me only one path that is beneficial for me to attain the highest good and I will follow that.

The principles of *karma yoga* are practical and useful for all of us. We experience confusion and strain related to our responsibilities and actions. Arjuna reaches a physical and emotional breakdown when confronted with a major civil war; an extremely challenging juxtaposition of time, place, and circumstances. The teaching of *karma yoga* in chapter III of the *Bhagavad Gītā* resolves his crisis by revealing the purpose and value of action. This teaching is not related with any creed, caste, country, or gender; it is a divine message for humankind. We all have the means and the responsibility to perform our duties effectively and with awareness, regardless of how we are challenged by life.

To resolve Arjuna's distress and guide him on a proper course of action, Krishna first enunciates an understanding of the self according to the principles of *Sāmkhya*.[16] *Karma yoga* is based on *Sāmkhya* because helpful

---

[16] See *Kapil's Sāmkhya Patanjali's Yoga* by Brahmrishi Vishvatma Bawra for a description of *sāmkhya*.

action relies on proper knowledge of our self and our position in life.

Our existence as human beings is the result of both energy and consciousness. Our physical and mental bodies are a projection of energy. This energy is infinite and unlimited. It is the source of our life and whatever is the source of life is divine. Energy appears in the form of our intellect, ego, mind, senses, and body. But according to *Sāmkhya* philosophy and Krishna, this energy is insentient. It is power and movement without intelligence or direction. *Sāmkhya* teaches that the expression of energy into form is inspired by a separate power: intelligence. This intelligence is called consciousness. Both energy and consciousness are eternal expressions of one source called supreme consciousness or *Brahman*.

Each individual has a causal seed, a causal form of energy. This causal level of individual existence is given various names according to different systems of philosophy. In *Sāmkhya* it is called intellect; in *Yoga* it is called *chitta*; and the *Upanishads* use the terms *sattva* or *brahma chakra*. It is a medium of energy and it adopts the qualities of consciousness. When supreme consciousness enlivens this medium, the self appears. Both energy, also called nature, and consciousness, also referred to as spirit, combine to form every individual being.

We are the result of the union of energy and consciousness. In our treatises, energy is our mother, consciousness is our father, and our soul or self is the child of these two divine parents. Both energy and consciousness are infinite, unlimited, and beyond our perception. They are beyond the grasp of our intellect, but we can be aware of their existence because we can experience their effects. Scientists tell us that energy is beyond perception. Scientific knowledge is based on evidence that can be measured and proven. If scientists cannot study energy directly, how can they prove it exists? Scientists see the effects of energy and by studying the effects, they learn about the cause. Therefore, scientists document the properties of invisible, ungraspable energy by evaluating its measurable and visible effects. This principle is known as cause and effect. By understanding the properties that exist in an effect, we can infer those qualities exist in the cause of that effect.

This principle was established by Kapil in ancient times and it is the foundation of *Sāmkhya* philosophy. Scientists know that energy, which is beyond description and perception, is the cause of matter. They describe energy as formless, weightless, limitless, and colorless; using negative adjectives because energy is beyond description and limitation. Energy is an infinite, unlimited, and all-pervasive power. It is the source of our life. We are all sitting here because of one source, and we are all receiving life energy in the form of oxygen from one source. All diversity is a projection of one infinite source of energy. Philosophy tells us that beyond energy is spirit. Using the principle of cause and effect, *Sāmkhya* states that not only energy, but also sentient consciousness resides in the source of our life.

What is the difference between energy and spirit? Energy is changeable: appearing and disappearing, manifesting and dissolving. Spirit is unchangeable. It is knowlegeful and enlightens all mediums formed by nature or energy. Spirit or consciousness is one absolute infinity, but appears in numerous forms or media. Even a little ant has its own *chitta* or medium. One infinite spirit enlightens the ant too. All beings exist with consciousness because of one supreme spirit. Both energy and consciousness are necessary for the formation of our life.

Each one of us has a highly developed system that adopts supreme consciousness and distributes life energy called *prāna*. In *Yoga* terminology, this system of distribution is called the *chakras*. At the top of our head is the highest and first *chakra*, the *brahma chakra*. When consciousness manifests in the *brahma chakra* two kinds of movement begin: breath and thought. Breathing is the effect of energy, and thinking is the effect of spirit. Breath and thought are the twin effects of our divine parents: energy and consciousness. Breath is the root cause of strength and strength gives us the ability to act. A person without strength cannot function. Consciousness is the root cause of thinking and planning, which inspire our actions. Breath does not plan anything. It has no ideas. Our ideas are projections of consciousness, and our strength is the result of breath or energy.

Every living being has both breath and thought at the root of their actions. Thought can be uplifting or it can be degrading. When we act according to knowledge, in the light of wisdom, then our action is *karma yoga*. If our action is motivated by our senses and thoughts of desire, fear, lust, or other emotions, then our action will not be *karma yoga* but *karma bhoga*.

Karma bhoga is action driven by the desire for a specific result. Every action gives results in the form of enjoyment or suffering. Helpful action brings enjoyment and with harmful action comes suffering. Even our enjoyment ends in suffering because the source of our enjoyment inevitably changes or passes away. Our actions are related with our motives and abilities. *Karma yoga* is action guided by wisdom and not desire. Krishna advises Arjuna to be a *karma yogi* and states, "A *yogi* is greater than one who does austerity, one who abandons action and pursues only knowledge, or one who relies on ritual. O Arjuna become a *yogi*."[17]

Krishna declares, "We cannot live a single moment without action. That is the destiny of every human being."[18] Our action is the projection of our strength and thoughts or emotions. Our strength is related with our breath and emotions are related with our heart. As humans, we cannot escape the activities of our breathing or our circulatory system. Our body acts to remain alive. Even renunciants continue to act, although they remove themselves from the challenges of day-to-day living in society. Activity is inescapable.

We have a soul, a body, and the fully developed means to perform duty. Action is our destiny so Krishna advises us to take action in the light of wisdom. *Karma yoga* establishes that every person has a head, heart, and hands. The head represents guiding knowledge and wisdom, the heart is the inspiring impulse of ideas, and hands are used to carry out the actions chosen by the head and heart. Helpful actions are identified in our head, chosen with our heart and completed with our hands. We should think and decide prior to acting, considering the result that will come from our action. Will this action be useful, leading me toward wholeness in my body and soul? Is this action

---

[17] *Bhagavad Gītā* VI/46.
[18] *Bhagavad Gītā* III/5.

prompted by desire for a specific object or experience, making me blind to the suffering that will follow?

Desire and emotion have a narrow focus. If we are compelled only by emotion then our effort leads to finite results. Saint Tulsidas wrote about the emotion of jealousy. He warned that if we feel jealous of someone, our mind and intellect do not work properly, and we are unable to see the virtues of the person triggering our jealousy. We can only see vices. When one emotion dominates us, we lose our ability to see the truth and we lose touch with our guiding wisdom. Emotions overpower our mind and we are unable to think about the consequences of our actions. We must first develop awareness or knowledge, then tame our emotions, and finally act wisely. We work from head to heart to hands. Krishna teaches that our authority extends only to the performance of action. We are never in control of the results of our actions. We must continue to act wisely regardless of whether we are rewarded or frustrated. Even a helpful action will be harmful to us if it is motivated by the desire for a specific gain. Inaction is also a harmful choice; we should not waste our abilities or opportunities to act wisely.[19]

Krishna advises Arjuna to use his wisdom and perform his duty. The third chapter begins with Arjuna's question: "O my Lord, if in your opinion wisdom is greater than action, why are you urging and guiding me to engage in this dreadful activity?"[20] War, and especially civil war, is terrible. Violence is not good work, so why are you

---

[19] *Bhagavad Gītā* II/47.
[20] *Bhagavad Gītā* III/1.

compelling me to kill these warriors and family members if you think wisdom is greater than action?

Arjuna is confused because he thinks that Krishna is praising knowledge over action, but also praising action over knowledge. He sees these as two separate choices with different sets of rules. This thinking is based on the prevalent ideas of his era: if an aspirant pursues knowledge alone then that person becomes a renunciant, ceasing participation in society; whereas a person choosing a life of action lives by the wisdom established in social rules of conduct. To Arjuna, it seems contradictory that Krishna is extolling wisdom and knowledge as a great path, while also advocating action and duty.

But Krishna states that wisdom without action and action without wisdom are both meaningless. If a person is wise, but remains silent and does not use wisdom to benefit society, then what benefit is this wisdom? If we refuse to act, then our wisdom is useless. Krishna is teaching that our wisdom must inspire action and we must use our ability to act in the light of wisdom. We must do some beneficial work for the welfare of all beings. Krishna also teaches that people who are full of energy, but act mindlessly invite suffering. Their efforts are in vain because they are not using their wisdom. Action without wisdom is the root cause of suffering.

Arjuna entreats Krishna, "Your teaching is creating confusion in my mind. Therefore, tell me only one path that is beneficial for me to attain the highest good and I will follow that." [21] Krishna teaches that we should not pursue wisdom alone, thinking good thoughts while

---

[21] *Bhagavad Gītā* III/2.

avoiding action. By itself, knowledge accomplishes nothing. Our thoughts must become deeds. Action reveals the value inherent in thought and wisdom.

We breathe and we think. Breath is the root cause of strength and thought is the root cause of ideas. When we engage our strength and our ideas in action, we are on the path of *karma yoga*. We cannot say that breath is better than thought or thought is better than breath. Without breath we would not be able to function and thinking would be impossible. And without thinking or knowledge, we would be unable to coordinate action. I do not think a selection can be made whether breath or thought is better. Both are needed and each has its proper value.

Krishna praises stable wisdom and enjoins Arjuna to act, causing Arjuna to ask: Which path is better? Arjuna's ambition is for the highest good, for perfection in life, and for emancipation. He wants to know the best path. Should he pursue the path of knowledge or the path of action? He wants one path that will assure him of achieving his goals.

August 26, 1998

III/3 My dear you are sinless. In the beginning of time, I taught two kinds of paths: one for those who are more analytical (*sāmkhya yoga*) and the other for those who are more active (*karma yoga*).

Arjuna's question is universal: What is the best path for gaining freedom from suffering? Krishna teaches about two paths, but points Arjuna toward *karma yoga*, the path that best suits his situation. To understand the principles of *karma yoga*, it is necessary to clearly understand the foundation of human life. Every one of us is the twofold expression of our supreme cause; we exist because the activity of nature or energy is stimulated by the light of spirit or consciousness.

Energy appears in the multiple levels of our being: physical, sensual, mental, egoistic, and intellectual. We experience life through these layers, which are all enlightened by consciousness. Both energy and consciousness are infinite. One infinite source appears in numerous names and forms, and each form is related with infinity. But we feel that we are limited and finite. We believe that we are limited because we are not aware of the ultimate truth: we are a projection of infinity. No one is separate from this infinite source because no effect can exist separate from its cause. As every effect resides in its cause, our existence is inseparable from our cause.

Energy causes the body, senses, mind, ego, and intellect to take shape, and supreme consciousness is the source of the soul. Although energy and consciousness are two expressions of one supreme cause, this philosophy is not dualistic because nature and spirit do not function separately. Energy acts in the light of supreme spirit. Energy is insentient and spirit is sentient. Our body, mind, and senses take form and become active in the light of our soul. If there is no soul present in the body, then all of the physical instruments cease to function. Spirit is the master of all the instruments of our body. We think of these tools as parts of one entity. If we are sitting alone in a room, and someone asks from behind the door, "Who is there?" we reply, "I am alone." We don't say, "Well, my body is here, my senses are here, my mind and intellect also." We do not count these as separate entities. These instruments have no separate existence from our self.

In the same way, we read in the *Vedas* that supreme spirit has two attributes. One is formful and the other is formless. Whatever appears in nature or manifests in and through nature is formful, and what is beyond nature, the enlightener of nature, is formless. We all are manifestations of supreme spirit. In this way, we all are one and our source of life is one. This is the foundation of our existence and the reason we are able to act in the world.

People reflect this twofold expression of oneness in different ways. Some are more intellectual, while others are more vigorous. These two kinds of expression are related with spirit and nature. Knowledge is the property of spirit and vigor is the property of energy.

Some people are energetic and active, always seeking outlets for their vigor. Others lean toward thinking and analyzing. But if knowledge and vigor are not used together, they have little value. Knowledge without action is pointless, and action without knowledge can be dangerous. When we act without proper knowledge, our actions are unlikely to be helpful to others or to ourselves. And if we think and plan, but never act on our ideas, we get nowhere. Knowledge becomes useful when it inspires action, and action becomes useful when it is informed by wisdom. Similarly, nature and spirit cannot manifest separately. It is the union of these two powers that generates all expressions of existence.

Supreme consciousness works with the divine power of nature to project into this universe. Without nature, spirit cannot do anything. Krishna states, "I manifest myself through my divine nature."[22] This universe could not exist as an expression of spirit alone, nor of nature alone. The universe exists because nature is inspired by spirit; energy takes form in the light of consciousness. Likewise our body, mind, ego, and intellect are part of the action of nature, and our soul or real self is the manifestation of consciousness. If we think but do not act, we are wasting our life; and if we act without knowledge or awareness, we are misusing our self.

Arjuna's question regarding one path toward the highest good in life is every person's question. We are often confused about our duty or the right course of action. We wonder what to do next. In our tradition when a person cannot find clarity, they approach a guru, a learned teacher, and ask for guidance. When Arjuna asks Krishna for a single clear path, he is asking for all of us. He wants a defined course of action that will give him both temporary relief and eternal peace.

---

[22] *Bhagavad Gītā* IV/6.

Krishna begins by telling Arjuna, "My dear you are sinless."[23] This indicates that Arjuna, or a person like him, is a proper student for divine knowledge. A sinful person will not have an ardent desire to know the truth behind this natural phenomenon. Sin is ignorance in the form of desire, temptation, and greed. It covers our mind and intellect, preventing us from seeing true knowledge, and making us the prey of delusion and infatuation. This leads to arrogance. A proud person will not approach a teacher for guidance. We say this kind of person believes there are only one and a half intellects in the world. The proud person has one and the other half is distributed among all other human beings. This attitude keeps them from seeking help on this divine path. Arjuna is sinless and a proper vessel for divine knowledge.

Krishna continues, "In the beginning of time, I taught two kinds of paths: one for those who are more analytical (*sāmkhya yoga*) and the other for those who are more active (*karma yoga*)."[24] People have different natures and they have different ways of thinking. Some tend to work in the light of the intellect and others are inspired by emotion.

The path of *sāmkhya* is analytical, the path of knowledge. It is for those who are more intellectually inclined. For these individuals, I teach renunciation of the fruit of action. Not to renounce action itself, but the fruit derived from action. These individuals should act without desire for personal gain. Performing action while detaching from the fruit of action does not create bondage.

---

[23] *Bhagavad Gītā* III/3.
[24] *Bhagavad Gītā* III/3.

These aspirants dwell on cause and effect, action and the result of action. They use their intellect and refine their thinking. They are not eager to act because their mode of mind is not drawn to action. They know that duties and action are related with the motivation or desire to engage in the world. If someone wants something, they must act in order to fulfill their desire. But if someone has no desire to achieve anything, then no action is required. Without motivation, action is unnecessary. But Krishna states that even people with no desire of their own should use their vigor, ability, and knowledge for the welfare of all beings.[25] Individuals who follow the path of knowledge should find activities that use their knowledge.

Perform action in order to worship the same self in all beings, rather than to gain recognition or worldly objects. *Sāmkhya yogis* are active, but they are detached from their action. They realize that action is nature acting with nature. They understand, "The attributes of nature are acting with the qualities of nature. I am not the doer, I am only the seer."[26] The real self is conscious awareness and it is seeing, not doing. The doer is part of nature. Nature performs all actions,[27] while spirit is the enlightener, seer, or knower.

When the sun shines, automatically a lotus opens. In the presence of sunlight the blossom is able to open. When the sun sets, the lotus closes. The sun is the enlightener and the lotus is the doer; in the same way, consciousness or the real self is the enlightener of our

---

[25] *Bhagavad Gītā* III/20.
[26] *Bhagavad Gītā* III/28.
[27] *Bhagavad Gītā* XIII/20.

instruments of action, while the instruments perform the actions.

Electricity provides the power for machines, which do the work. Electricity is not part of the machines, but electricity causes the machines to work. Without electricity a machine is useless and inactive. As a machine cannot function without electricity; in the same way our senses and body cannot act without consciousness. A *sāmkhya yogi* is aware of the real position of self as the seer and knows that nature is doing and self is observing. "He is fully aware about nature and spirit and understands all movement is part of nature, and spirit only enlightens and observes."[28] In this way, a *sāmkhya yogi* remains detached from all actions while performing actions.

The alternate path is *karma yoga*. *Karma yoga* suits the *yogi* who is embedded in the world of action. They are vigorous people whose natures demand action. If *karma* is the cause of bondage, how can a *yogi* be busy and remain free? Krishna explains that it is not action that creates bondage, but the motive behind the action. A *karma yogi* performs action as the means to worship Godhead. Action serves divinity.

"A *karma yogi* acts for pleasing the Lord."[29] This person realizes the supreme cause in the world of action. This is a *yogi*: a realized soul who knows one supreme cause inspires nature's movement. Movement causes the manifestation of this natural phenomenon and all other actions. Therefore, the *karma yogi* acts because Godhead inspires activity. A *karma yogi* acts while thinking of Godhead and worshipping Godhead. Action itself is not

---

[28] *Bhagavad Gītā* V/8.
[29] *Bhagavad Gītā* XVIII/46.

the cause of bondage. Desire for and attachment to the fruit or results of action is what causes harm.

When we act on behalf of Godhead with the motive of worship, then our action will not bind us. But if our mind is focused on what we will gain from our action, then we are not free. Action without attachment to the fruit of action is liberating.

Action is action, whether it is the movement of the mind, senses or body. "Sleeping, eating, thinking, moving, talking, or drinking; any action alone is not the cause of liberation or bondage. *Yogis* are able to act while remaining free from attachment to worldly affairs because they know that action occurs when the tools of nature interact with the objects of nature."[30]

When we practice *karma yoga*, we have no intention regarding the fruit of action. Our intention is related with Godhead and achieving the highest good. *Karma yogis* are aware that all movements of the body and senses are part of nature.[31] Practicing in this way, we become free from *karma*. Krishna states, "Vigorous people achieve my divine grace and love by doing action for me. They perform action for me not for their own individual self. Their motive is not selfish; they are without self-interest."[32]

On the path of *karma yoga*, we use our vigor, power, and strength for pleasing Godhead, and our actions become fruitful for all beings. A *sāmkhya yogi* also acts for the welfare of others, but there is a slight difference between the two paths. On the path of *karma yoga*, we act on behalf of Godhead and our actions in the world are

---

[30] *Bhagavad Gītā* V/8.
[31] *Bhagavad Gītā* XIII/20.
[32] *Bhagavad Gītā* XI/55.

offerings to the divine. *Sāmkhya yogis* are rooted in the infinite self and direct their actions for the welfare of all beings. Clearly, whatever one does on behalf of Godhead will benefit other beings, but the mind of the *karma yogi* is related with a personal God. The result is the same because both kinds of practitioners are detached from the fruit of action. A *karma yogi* is free from the bondage of action and delights in a personal realization of Godhead, while the *sāmkhya yogi's* delight is in the one self indwelling all beings. "The aspirant whose delight is in the self, whose satisfaction is in the self, and who is content in the self; for this person the need to act does not exist. His or her motivation for action is the welfare of all beings."[33] Both paths lead to the highest good.

Consciousness is stable and without movement; while energy changes and moves. The *yogi* joins head and heart, knowledge and vigor, together in the light of supreme consciousness. In this way individual consciousness rises above the mind and joins with infinite supreme consciousness. This is an integrated path. Life energy or *prāna* becomes one with the supreme cause and perfection in life is attained.

This is the process of *yoga*. *Yogis* join head and heart, thinking and feeling, together, always focusing on the supreme cause. A *yogi* acts on behalf of the supreme cause, serving the divine in the formful, personified form of a deity, or as the formless supreme self indwelling all beings. Knowing we cannot survive a single moment without action, a *yogi* acts. Both the followers of *sāmkhya* and *karma* are detached and tread the divine path. Their methods

---

[33] *Bhagavad Gītā* III/17.

differ, but both paths lead to the highest level of consciousness and emancipation. On one path, the intellect leads the journey, and on the other path, the heart guides the way.

One should not think that a *karma yogi* has no knowledge or that a *sāmkhya yogi* has no vigor. Everyone has head and heart, knowledge and vigor, consciousness and energy. Our life is a combination of both and we cannot create a division between the two. We would not exist without both of them. They are the essential elements of life.

Karma yogis use vigor, strength, power, and energy. They do practices to receive divine energy, which they use to worship the divine. *Sāmkhya yogis* use their intellect and wisdom, developing intuition to realize supreme truth, and act in the light of supreme consciousness. These two paths are from ancient times given for the different manifestations of human nature. We all have knowledge and vigor. Combining knowledge and action in daily practice is the ideal path. Thinking about these teachings without putting them into practice prevents progress, and acting in the world without divine guidance takes us in circles. Join knowledge with action, following the *sāmkhya yoga* path or the *karma yoga* path. Both lead to the supreme goal.

August 27, 1998

III/4 A human does not attain the highest state of release from the binding effect of *karma* by withholding action or by renouncing action alone.

Human beings and other animals fill their stomachs, satisfy their thirst, defend themselves, reproduce and care for their progeny, but humans have intellect, the highest faculty given by Godhead. With our intellect we can contemplate our goals and engineer our plans. Our vital force and our intelligence give us a vast capacity for resourceful, thoughtful action. Movement belongs to nature, our bodies are part of nature, and action is a fundamental aspect of being human. We must act, but if we do not act with our intelligence in the light of wisdom, we squander our unique abilities and waste our lives. When our vital forces are guided by wisdom we can effectively perform our duties to benefit all beings.

We are given five cognitive senses, five active senses, five primordial elements, mind, ego, life energy, and wisdom.[34] When we use our faculties in the light of wisdom for the benefit of all beings, we are divine. When we use our gifts to selfishly accumulate, we are demonic. If we believe in limitation and individuality, we see diversity everywhere, which leads to comparison, insecurity, jealousy and greed. Feeling deficient, we use our energy

---

[34] Our five cognitive senses are the ears, skin, eyes, tongue and nose; our five active senses are the mouth, hands, legs, and generative and eliminative organs; and our bodies are made up of five primordial elements: space, air, fire, water and earth.

and intelligence to seek among worldly affairs for temporary satisfaction. Demonic people get caught in an endless cycle of desire, which ultimately leads to grief.

If we turn our face toward unity, then we realize the source of our intelligence and vigor. We begin to realize infinity within our self. In infinity, we experience unity and know that diversity is an appearance; it is not the truth. This frees us from our sense of lack and compulsion for comparison. We achieve this liberated state by turning our senses and our intellect from outside to inside.

Even after achieving a peaceful internal state, we remain active in the external world. When we attain a state of desireless happiness, without temptation for worldly objects and affairs, we continue performing *karma*. We are blessed with the gifts of Godhead, the instruments of action, and action is our destiny. It is our right and duty to act, but action is not for personal gain, it is for the welfare of others. When we act without seeking certain results, then our actions are not binding, and we end the cycle of desire and despair. Krishna states, "We have the right to action alone."[35] A farmer produces crops and countless creatures benefit, including birds, insects and unknown organisms in the soil. In the same way our actions influence many beings. We are unaware of the full impact of our actions, we cannot control any outcome, and we should not think our actions remain contained within our personal motives.

Krishna teaches, "A human does not attain the highest state of release from the binding effect of *karma* by withholding action or by renouncing action alone."[36]

---

[35] *Bhagavad Gītā* II/47.
[36] *Bhagavad Gītā* III/4.

When we act without attachment to the results of action, we reach a higher state of consciousness, which is above all action. In this state we know we are the non-doer, and we observe the movements of nature. As the observer, we are fully aware and established in the self. In this higher state of practice, we realize our unity with Godhead and understand that all activity is related with nature.

Action is nature's movement. Nature appears in the form of energy as electrons, protons, and neutrons, which compose atoms. Atoms combine into molecules and matter, from which our bodies appear. Our bodies and all movements are the projection and property of nature working in the light of supreme consciousness. Movement is a property of nature just as light is a property of the sun and heat is a property of fire.

We cannot stop our action. We are unable to stop nature's movement. We are not nature's master. We are part and parcel of nature. Krishna tells, "My material nature appears in eightfold form: earth, water, fire, air, space, mind, intellect, and ego. This is my inferior nature and it is different from the self, which is superior, and by which this universe is maintained."[37] Nature projects into these forms. When we live in a body and adopt these means, we are living in nature and nature acts. We cannot stop it. Even when we think we are not doing anything, we are acting by holding our position. We are doing mental work rather than physical work. We are deciding not to act.

Work is not related with the body alone. It is also related with speech and thought. When we choose not to

---

[37] *Bhagavad Gītā* VII/4 & 5.

do something, and we refrain from action, we are doing mental work. Whether we act internally or externally, subtly or obviously, it is all action. At times our subtle, inner actions are more powerful and dangerous than our physical outer actions. We may internalize stress, which makes us sick; or we may allow our thinking to become so disturbed that we make harmful decisions. Krishna is telling us that we do not achieve the highest state by resisting action. We are compelled to act using our instruments in nature, guided by our self, which resides in consciousness.

The happiness we seek is the bliss of supreme consciousness. This is not attained by renouncing activity. Mental effort, including meditation, is a kind of activity. If we renounce all activity, then how is it possible to do higher practices? All spiritual effort is action and we cannot achieve perfection without effort. This is why Krishna tells us that we cannot achieve the highest state by resisting action. Although the highest state is without movement, it is achieved with effort.

In the highest state we become desireless. "For those practitioners who are eager to attain the highest state action is the means. And for those practitioners who have attained *yoga* tranquility is the means."[38] Action is the effort to gain perfection. In *yoga*, tranquility is a state without disturbance or movement. One who becomes free from limitations, attachments and desires attains perfection and is called a *siddha*.

Siddha means perfection in life, and *siddhas* are free from the fear of death, ignorance and doubt. When we are

---

[38] *Bhagavad Gītā* VI/3.

free from the fear of death, we achieve immortality. The signs of a perfected being are doubtless knowledge, lustless love, and desireless service. *Siddhas* are fulfilled. They are one with infinite, supreme consciousness. They have no desire and are liberated from the feeling of being the doer. Though they perform action, they understand it is the qualities of nature acting and they are the seer of that action. Just as action continues in nature in the light of Godhead, their action continues in the light of their wisdom.

No one can live a single moment without performing action. Without action, we cannot complete our journey in this body. We must eat and drink, sleep and awaken. It is impossible to be free from action, but it is not action that creates bondage. Attachment with the fruit of action causes bondage. Expectation of results makes us slaves, not action itself. We are able to perform many actions without attachment to their results and these actions do not bind us. We pass along roads and enjoy the natural world, taking in the scenery whether it is beautiful or ugly. We remain the observer, free to enjoy the movement of nature.

August 28, 1998

III/5 It is impossible to live without action. We are forced into action, even against our will, by the attributes which are inherent in material nature.

III/6 If one sits restraining his organs of action, but brooding over the objects of these senses with a deluded mind, this one is a hypocrite.

III/7 If one uses the senses with wisdom, remaining detached from the objects of the senses, the one practicing this *yoga* of action is great.

Our ability to reason makes us unique. With our reason, we are able to discern the difference between uplifting practices and degrading behavior. When our mind and senses are guided by discrimination and wisdom, then these instruments are useful. They provide information about experience and allow us to interact with the world. But when the mind and senses are led by emotion and desire, then the mind hankers to experience the objects of the senses and we use our instruments in destructive ways.

We cannot live a single moment without action.[39] The instruments of the mind and the senses constantly interact and collect information from the environment. Therefore, it is critical that we use our discrimination to process and assess this information. When our mind becomes attached to external experiences, valuing them above our own self, desire leads us into the cycle of action, satiation, and a

---

[39] *Bhagavad Gītā* III/5.

desire to repeat the experience. This leads to frustration and increased desire. We become the slave of our desires, running in circles and blind to the possibility of freedom. It is not the activity of collecting experiential information that causes bondage, but our misplaced values and pursuit of transitory experiences. Nature continuously moves and transforms. If energy stopped moving, the projected universe, including our body, would no longer exist. We are alive on earth because of energy's movement. Our cells continuously regenerate. With each breath, we receive fresh oxygen and discharge impurities, and our circulating blood nourishes our system. "It is impossible to live without action. We are forced into action, even against our will, by the attributes which are inherent in material nature."[40] Our intellect, mind, and senses are under the influence of these attributes, called the three *gunas*. If *sattoguna* – the quality of illumination – prevails, then our actions are beneficial for all beings. When *rajoguna* – the attribute of agitation – dominates, then we become selfish and harm ourselves and others. Under the power of *tamoguna*, which is inertia, our life is useless.

To ease human suffering, systems of thought developed regarding the performance of action. These systems emphasized two primary paths. On one, the main idea was that action causes bondage; therefore aspirants should renounce action to achieve emancipation. The other system prescribed rules for performing action in order to achieve positive results, including the attainment of heaven. Complex rules and duties were developed for living among family and society, and sacrifices were

---

[40] *Bhagavad Gītā* III/5.

offered to the natural divine elements. The complexity of these rules came under the power of the literate classes, who took advantage of common people and encouraged superstition.

The *Bhagavad Gītā* takes a unique stance: we can live in the world and gain emancipation through the performance of action. We can realize ultimate truth, achieve perfection in life, and be free from bondage by understanding and rising above the cause of bondage. Krishna explains, "Your authority extends only to the performance of action. Obtaining or not obtaining the fruit is never within your control. Therefore, do not perform action with an acquisitive motive, desiring a particular fruit. Nor should one insist on not performing action."[41]

Action itself is not the cause of bondage. We become bound by our motives and desires. Nature is insentient. It does not have a motive. As elements of energy combine and recombine; nature changes and transforms. Insentient nature cannot bind a sentient being. The house we live in cannot bind us. It is inanimate. Inanimate objects can not act against us. In the same way, our body does not bind us. Nature is the cause of action, but it is not the cause of bondage.

Krishna tells us to understand the root cause of our bondage and suffering, and work to weed out this cause. Our attachment to the qualities we receive from the objects of the senses is the root cause of our enslavement. Our mind and senses do not cause bondage. They receive and process useful information. It is when our ego

---

[41] *Bhagavad Gītā* II/47.

attaches to the qualities of experience and defines the self by these qualities of nature that we become bound.

This attachment comes from ignorance, a lack of distinction between the qualities of the objects and the qualities of our self. Delusion and infatuation with external experience causes our suffering. Once we clearly differentiate the qualities of nature from our self and our source, then ignorance and attachment end. In ancient times, many great and wealthy kings were philosophers. King Janaka, Yudisthira, and Krishna were kings of India who lived in luxury, but who understood the proper value of all objects in relation to the self. They performed their duties as rulers, used necessary objects, and remained free.

We can avail ourselves of what is useful. It is possible to use objects and relate to people without causing suffering. The value we place on people and things and the desire to cling, accumulate and hoard are what harm and bind us. A person who lives in a rented house enjoys the benefits of the house, but does not feel the burden and responsibility of ownership. If we feel ownership of any material or living thing, then we feel attached. A gardener who is working for someone else may plant, nurture, and enjoy the benefits of gardening. The gardener is able to work hard while knowing he or she is not the owner of the garden. In the same way, this universe is a beautiful garden. We can tend the garden, and see and enjoy its benefits, knowing we are not the owner. If we understand that every thing is a projection of divine nature and every person is a manifestation of the supreme cause, automatically we gain detachment because our sense of ownership ends.

The *Īsa Upanishad* declares, "This world is pervaded by supreme Godhead. Each part of nature is permeated by that divine power. We are not the owner. Remember whose wealth this is."[42] Every effect comes from its cause, belongs to its cause, and returns to its cause. All effects eventually merge back into their source. We are not the cause of any objects; they are all projections of divine power. When we become fully aware of the cause of this universe, our cause, we become free from attachment and gain emancipation.

We have the right to use nature. Oxygen is most precious and valuable for us; we cannot live without breathing this divine energy. We must use oxygen, but we cannot claim that oxygen belongs to us. Whatever is subtle or divine does not belong to any one person. Everything that exists in this world is a projection of the divine power of nature, and when we understand this, we become free from attachment.

We must be careful how we control our cognitive and active senses. "If one sits restraining his organs of action, but brooding over the objects of these senses with a deluded mind, this one is a hypocrite.[43] If one uses the senses with wisdom, remaining detached from the objects of the senses, the one practicing this *yoga* of action is great."[44]

In Krishna's teaching, the first type of aspirant resists performing duty. These people close their eyes, but see their fantasies; close their ears, but think about melodious sounds; and close their mouths, but crave food. They

---

[42] *Īsa Upanishad* 2.
[43] *Bhagavad Gītā* III/6.
[44] *Bhagavad Gītā* III/7.

dwell on acquiring and enjoying the objects of senses, while controlling their active senses. They give the appearance of being masterly, yet their minds are busy with the qualities of the objects even in the absence of the objects. Krishna tells us these individuals are deluded. Their restraint is in vain. They give a show of being desireless and detached, while their minds crave and remain active; outside they appear peaceful while inside they are full of disturbances. These individuals do not bring their thought, speech or action into alignment and they are not *yogis*.

Regardless of where our body is, we exist where our mind exists. We may sit in a holy place, but if we are thinking about sensual enjoyment, we do not gain the benefits of our holy surroundings. Likewise, we may be surrounded by temptations, but if our mind has no craving, we are free. Our individual body does not endow us with unique qualities; it is our intellect that gives us superior potential. If we are desireless while using our senses, we are not bound by them. "But if we allow our mind to follow our wandering senses, then our reason is carried away as wind carries a boat in water."[45] When the mind is not anchored in the true self, the mind is drawn toward the objects of the senses and we are at the mercy of our desires. This causes our suffering.

Our present life is the result of our previous actions and our future will be the result of our current behavior. Using all our means of action while acting without attachment brings us to the highest state. If our mind and reason follow the objects of the senses, our experience

---

[45] *Bhagavad Gītā* II/67.

leads to pleasure and pain as the objects come and go. Our thoughts and actions should be guided by our wisdom. In the light of wisdom, our vigor and effort carry us on the divine path and we achieve our highest goal. We become free while acting with wisdom.

August 29, 1998

III/8 We should perform action according to our abilities and capabilities. This is our prescribed duty; it is better to perform action than to avoid action. Even the maintenance of our body requires action.

We all want to be free from ignorance, insecurity, and the fear of death. This aim is the same for all humans regardless of our ability or capacity. Even though we all have different levels of intellectual ability, vitality and strength, we want to be wise, vigorous and immortal. What we did in our past structures our current circumstances, skills and capabilities; and we establish our future abilities and potential with our current behavior. We need to know what we can do in the present that will bring us toward eternal fulfillment and peace. For this reason, Krishna teaches *karma yoga*.

"We should perform action according to our abilities and capabilities. This is our prescribed duty; it is better to perform action than to avoid action. Even the maintenance of our body requires action."[46] When we work according to our ability and capacity, we are performing our prescribed duty. In Sanskrit, this is called *dharma*. Nowadays, people think about rights rather than duties. In order to fulfill our duty, we need to use the skills we have, and develop our abilities with disciplined effort. This is required for success in life. If we use our active senses to do our work, while also using our intellect to

---

[46] *Bhagavad Gītā* III/8.

control our mind and cognitive senses, we are performing *karma yoga*. Motive is the root of *karma yoga*. If we want to be both useful and free, we choose divinity as our inspiration and we perform our duty to the best of our ability, while remaining desireless and detached.

If the same work is driven by desire and expectation, rather than the aspiration to improve our skills and develop our self, it is *karma bhoga*. In *karma bhoga*, our cognitive senses compel us to strive in order to obtain the objects of the senses. Hearing melodious song, tasting delicious food, or seeing beautiful scenery compels us to follow our senses so that we can repeat the experience. We gain brief satisfaction, but do not achieve lasting peace and happiness. We temporarily enjoy, but we do not find tranquility; our transient pleasure only creates more thirst in our mind.

Greed is never satiated. Those who have thousands want millions; those with millions want billions; and those with billions want ultimate power. Desire always increases and is never satisfied, but our capabilities are limited. We cannot fulfill unlimited desire with our limited means. Ultimately, endless desire leaves us feeling deficient and miserable.

In this philosophy, our world of action is called *karma loka*. *Sāmkhya* tells us that there are five levels of existence lower than human life, and eight *lokas* or worlds higher than human life.[47] The five stages lower than human life are projections of *tamoguna*: mammal, bird, reptile, insect,

---

[47] For further discussion on this topic, see Sutra 18, "Fourteen Stages of Evolution of Beings," *Kapil's Sāmkhya Patanjali's Yoga* by B. V. Bawra; and "Evolution, Transmigration and Perfection," *The Eternal Soul* by B.V. Bawra.

and vegetation. The eight higher levels are projections of *sattoguna* and these are called divine *lokas*. A *loka* is a "perceptible world." When evolution occurs, the first manifestation of nature is cosmic intellect. When this cosmic medium becomes enlivened by supreme consciousness, it is called *brahmā*. The first *sattvic* or divine world is called *brahmā loka*. The second projection is cosmic ego, and the related *loka* is *prājapāti loka*. The third is cosmic mind, related with the subtle world of *indra loka*. After these come the cognitive senses which align with *deva loka*. *Deva* means divine. The cognitive senses are called divine because they enlighten the material objects with consciousness. *Pitri loka* follows and is the place of desires, also called the place of the ancestors. Our desires become the root cause of our birth and death. Next comes *gāndharva loka*, the world of sensual pleasures. The root word *gāndharve* means that which catches the objects of senses, in other words, our active senses. The two lowest *lokas* where human souls travel between lives, are called *rāksasa loka* and *paishācha loka*. *Rāksasas* are infatuated with power and use force to meet their needs, and *paishāchas* use trickery, deceit, and cleverness to attain their goals. Following the eight levels of the divine world, there is one projection of *rajoguna*, human life.

Deities live in the heavenly or divine worlds, and the souls who perform virtuous works in human life enjoy the results of their activities in the divine spheres.[48] Once the results of previous virtue finish, a soul returns to *karma loka*. People who are sinful suffer by returning to life in the lower species. Human life is the result of action, both

---

[48] *Bhagavad Gītā* IX/21.

good and bad. Our body is said to be the field of activity, *karma kshetra*.[49] We are only able to perform our duty in this world; human life provides our only chance to develop our abilities and achieve the highest good. In the divine worlds, we are unable to perform action for self-improvement; deities and souls are busy with enjoyment. The lower species do not have the means to achieve the highest good. The actions of these plants and animals are prompted by natural phenomena and instinct. Only humans are free to perform actions that lead to ultimate truth.

Karma has four categories: *karma, sukarma, satkarma* and *vikarma*. *Karma* is the duty related with our position and abilities within our family, society, and nation. All of us have responsibilities and prescribed duties related with our circumstances. In order for society to function well, we need to perform our duties well. *Sukarma* is virtuous work motivated by the desire to achieve heavenly enjoyment in the divine sphere. *Satkarma* is action inspired by the goal of emancipation or ultimate truth. *Satkarma* makes us free from the cycle of birth and death. *Karma yoga* is *satkarma*. Whether we are taking care of our responsibilities or performing religious work, we must rid ourselves of the desire for the fruit of our actions. The last type of *karma* is *vikarma*, wrong action, which should be avoided. Destructive actions carry us away from ultimate truth and cause suffering. Do not confuse *satkarma* with *sukarma*. *Satkarma* is *karma yoga*, while *sukarma* is not. *Sukarma* is virtuous work and prayers, prompted by the desire to enjoy the subtle pleasures of heaven or for

---

[49] *Bhagavad Gītā* XIII/1.

gaining a specific opportunity in life. The work of *karma yoga* is *satkarma*; it is neither virtuous nor non-virtuous. It is beyond both and leads us to the abode of eternal bliss. We need to perform our duties related with this body and the world, using our abilities and capabilities for the welfare of all beings on behalf of Godhead.

Action without personal motive or desire for the fruit is *satkarma*. If we tend to be more vigorous and devotional, we can use our attributes to perform action while thinking of Godhead. If we are intellectually inclined, we are able to perform duty for the welfare of all beings, purifying our mind to achieve ultimate truth. Both of these methods are *satkarma*.

Foundation of *Karma Yoga*
August 30, 1998

III/9 Aside from action for the purpose of sacrifice, this world is bound by action. Perform action for this purpose Arjuna, abandoning attachment and hope for the fruit.

III/10 When humankind came into existence, this method of sacrifice was developed by Lord *Prajapati* in order to sustain human life. *Prajapati* said, "By this sacrifice may you grow. May this be the means for you to satisfy all of your desires."

When our actions are directed toward fulfilling the cravings of our senses, we may briefly enjoy ourselves, but our misguided actions always lead to suffering. Nature is changeable, and transitory objects will never give us eternal peace and happiness. Nature is bound by time, place and circumstances. If we seek enjoyment and security from anything in the natural world, whatever we value today will change tomorrow, causing us suffering and insecurity. Any happiness we experience is limited by settings and conditions that are beyond our control. Our temporary enjoyment always ends in disappointment. To find lasting peace and happiness, we must turn inward. Our eternal soul is unchangeable and ever-present; it is the abode of peace and happiness. When our actions are dedicated to spiritual development and the upliftment of our soul, they lead to eternal bliss.

The motives behind our actions either keep us bound in the cycle of birth and death or lead to our emancipation. The philosophy of *karma yoga* directs us to perform action while understanding its binding or liberating potential. When we relate our actions with a higher purpose, we move toward emancipation. In the first eight verses of chapter III, Krishna describes the philosophy behind *karma yoga*. As humans, we have a body, senses, a mind, an ego and our intellect, which are all projections of nature. As movement is the quality of nature, these natural instruments are changeable and unstable. Their fluctuations and desires often control us, and it is challenging to discipline their functions. We are often forced into action against our will. The enlightener of these instruments is our real self or soul. Our soul is above all of these instruments and the movement of nature. Yet our soul becomes attached to the instruments it enlightens. Because of this attachment we suffer in life and we fear dying, as we cycle through birth and death. Destructive attachments may cause our soul to inhabit lower life forms, but with disciplined effort, our soul continues to achieve a human form and gradually attains emancipation. When our soul is in a human body, we are most fortunate because we have our intellect and this gives us the opportunity to attain the highest truth. Intellect is the greatest gift of divinity, and we should use this instrument to analyze and discern what is beneficial for our life. In this way, we use our intelligence and energy to free us from the cycle of birth and death and reach eternal peace and happiness.

In the next verse, III/9, Krishna begins teaching the foundation underlying *karma yoga*. He first gives Arjuna the established doctrine of sacrifice: "Aside from action for the purpose of sacrifice, this world is bound by action."

He continues with the philosophy of *karma yoga*: "Perform action for this purpose Arjuna, abandoning attachment and hope for the fruit."[50] Krishna urges us to act according to our developed abilities and capacity, performing our actions without attachment to the rewards. Anything we do on behalf of divinity brings freedom. We strive to act in the spirit of sacrifice. We detach from any expectations or hopes for specific results, both in this life and after death, acting with no desire to gain heaven. Everything we do with a selfish motive to satisfy our senses causes bondage. Krishna encourages us to develop our devotion to divinity, to be inspired by divinity, and to offer our selfless action as a sacrifice to divinity, the practice of *yagya*.

Yagya has a very great meaning. It is the true form of sacrifice: worshipping divinity, receiving divine energy, and then offering this divine energy in service to others. First, we meditate on divinity to receive divine energy in our own life. Then we gather this divine energy, allowing it to enliven our faculties so that we may offer this energy for the welfare of all beings. In this way we perform *yagya*. Unfortunately, a limited understanding of this process developed over time. Sacrifice came to be related with the offering of an oblation into fire. Various offerings were made with the intent to gain material or heavenly benefits. For example, farmers offered grain into a sacrificial fire, hoping this would bring a bountiful new crop. In time these practices developed to include the killing and offering of animals. This is not the real meaning of *yagya* or sacrifice. *Yagya* is meditating on our divine source and

---

[50] *Bhagavad Gītā* III/9.

the expression of divine facilities that surround us, and offering up our efforts to provide selfless service guided by these divine facilities.

Divine facilities work continuously and offer their qualities to support and aid our lives. Earth, water, fire, air, and space are all divine qualities. They are projections of divine energy. Each divine faculty is associated with a special quality. Earth has the quality of forgiveness. I do not think anyone could bear what the earth tolerates, while continuing to provide nourishment for our food. Water quenches the thirst of all beings. Fire gives light and life. Air offers life energy and makes it possible for us to be active. And space provides a place for us.

All these divine faculties support our lives. Each has its own virtue. We should not try to accumulate and hoard these qualities, but encourage their use for the welfare of all beings. If we receive the benefit of these divine faculties, but use and enjoy them for our own self rather than for the welfare of others, then we are stealing these gifts. Whatever we do with selfish interests imprisons us rather than making us free. Krishna teaches that whatever we do for the welfare of all is uplifting, *satkarma*, and whatever we do selfishly causes bondage and ends in suffering.

Krishna advises performing action for the welfare of all beings on behalf of Godhead. In this way, we protect ourselves from pride. If we act solely for the benefit of society, then pride creeps into our life. We think we are the doer, we own our accomplishments, and we earn the approval of others. We have all seen people who perform good works while inflated with self-importance. Even though their actions are beneficial for society, in the end their actions bind them. We should be detached, while guided by divinity, acting on behalf of divinity.

"When humankind came into existence, this method of sacrifice was developed by Lord *Prajapati*[51] in order to sustain human life. *Prajapati* said, 'By this sacrifice may you grow. May this be the means for you to satisfy all of your desires.'"[52] As humans, we have a special place in this universe, and we are considered to be the image of the supreme being. Godhead performed sacrifice in order to project this universe, and taught us this same method for performing action in the spirit of sacrifice in order to bring forth new generations and to fulfill our inner demand for lasting happiness.

There are five levels of sacrifice, called oblations, discussed in the *Chāndogya Upanishad*. The five oblations describe the sacrificial process that is necessary for human birth. First, the supreme being offers itself into the divine abode of the sun. Second, the sun offers itself into the clouds, which become the rain that descends onto the earth. Third, the earth, with rain and the sun's heat, sprouts food that is offered into a man's body, where, fourth, semen is created. The semen is offered into a woman's body to begin a new life.[53] Humankind is the

---

[51] According to the Vedic tradition, *Prājapāti* is a name given to the creator. From this level of manifestation, the deities and worlds sprang forth. After the gods and worlds came into existence, *Prājapātii* was concerned with how this universe would be maintained. He performed austere sacrificial practices for a thousand years, worshipping the supreme Lord, thus establishing the method of sacrificial activity as the way to maintain and support all activity. *Mahabharata* 340.38-62.
[52] *Bhagavad Gītā* III/10.
[53] *Chāndogya Upanishad* V.9.1.

result of these offerings and continues by this sacrificial process. We offer our life energy to conceive offspring, and humankind continues. This sacrificial process begins with the supreme being, and it is ongoing, teaching us the way to endeavor from generation to generation toward ultimate truth and lasting happiness.

Sacrifice is based on receiving and offering. We are always taking in and giving out. We receive oxygen and release carbon dioxide. We receive food and water to sustain our body and we give off waste. Air, water and food give us the energy we need to be active and continue the process of evolution. We do not live a single moment without giving and receiving. We receive many kinds of nourishment and we discharge a special energy from our bodies. This energy vibrating and surrounding our body is called our aura.

The kind of energy we give off is determined by our motives, which also influence the vibratory color of the energy we discharge. If our motives are pure, we discharge uplifting white energy. If our aura is dark, we are discharging negative energy, indicating physical and mental impurity and selfish motives. Every being receives and emits energy. The energy we discharge is influenced by our thoughts. We can think in positive and generous ways or negative and selfish ways. Our pure or polluted mind influences the vibrations surrounding our body and impacts our internal and external environment.

Without giving, we cannot receive. If we do not discharge carbon dioxide we cannot receive oxygen. And if we do not offer our focused effort we cannot receive the wisdom of ultimate truth. Unfortunately, these ideas are no longer understood or valued. We want to take and keep, but do not want to give and sacrifice. The prevalence of selfishness among humans threatens the sacrificial process and the happiness intended for humankind. This is why we see so much suffering and struggle.

When we accumulate and hoard, we bring struggle and suffering into our lives. The more we amass, the more we fuel our endless desire and greed. If we have no way to satisfy our greed, we may steal from those who have more. It is a refreshing relief to simply use our share, which includes preparing wisely for our future, while helping others in society. This eases the struggle for ourselves and uplifts others, bringing happiness. This is the divine process and intent behind *yagya*. *Yagya* is not intended for personal gain, but for developing our ability to receive divinity and share divinity with others. For this reason, *karma yoga* has been taught since ancient times. At the heart of *karma yoga* is the understanding of sacrifice. To live a life of peace and happiness, we do not act for personal gain. We sacrifice our energy, wealth, ability, power and vigor; offering whatever we have for the benefit of all because we are all the projection of one supreme being.

August 31, 1998

III/11 By this process of sacrifice, we nourish the gods and the gods nourish us. By nourishing each other, we attain the highest benefit.

In the previous verse, Krishna tells that when humankind was born, the Lord developed and taught *yagya*, the process of sacrifice, as the means to multiply and prosper. First, we must give what we have to offer, and in this way we are able to receive. Prosperity is the result of sacrifice. A farmer sows seeds in the earth and then harvests crops. If a farmer stores the entire harvest, rather than sowing seeds for the future, the stores will run out and nothing will be left. Sacrifice is the act of offering. We sacrifice what we have and receive something greater. A businessman must invest money to receive profits. A laborer sacrifices strength and receives money in return. We offer our knowledge, ability, strength, and whatever we have, and the result is that we gain from what we give. If we hope to have a child, we must offer our life energy. We only receive by offering what we have. Everywhere this divine law applies. Sacrifice was created along with humankind. It is the means for fulfilling our needs and achieving our desires.

When sacrificial practices were developed, sacrifices were made to the gods, the divine powers of nature that support all life, such as earth, wind or fire. A form of these practices remains beneficial today. First, we meditate on the divine powers; then we collect divine energy from these powers; and finally we offer this energy to others.

"By this process of sacrifice, we nourish the gods and the gods nourish us. By nourishing each other, we attain the highest benefit."[54] These sustaining practices bring happiness into our lives and throughout creation. Every action causes a reaction. When a person does something helpful, the divine powers come to support and nourish this activity. In this way, the divine powers are cherished and we are blessed with happiness.

We all come from the same ancestors. Different cultures have spread from one origin. Our ancestors led their lives according to the Vedic teachings given by the ancient seers. These teachings spread among many cultures and were adopted into varying forms. The performance of five kinds of sacrifice, related to the five primordial elements, was among the earliest teachings and practices.

We all use the primordial elements of earth, water, fire, air, and space, and our behaviors impact the elements of nature. Knowingly or unknowingly, we cause pollution and harm to the earth and countless creatures. How is it possible to be free from the results of these actions? The five kinds of sacrifice taught in the Vedas offer a process for healing our damage. The first practice is to offer some symbols of earth, such as rice or spices, into a sacrificial fire. The next action is to recite holy scriptures and *mantras* as the name of God. The third method is to acknowledge and pay homage to our ancestors who protected and passed on knowledge. The fourth offering is to care for guests and help others in need. And the last practice is to protect the earth's resources, including birds, animals,

---

[54] *Bhagavad Gītā* III/11.

insects, plants, water and soil. These efforts helped to purify and strengthen the environment in ancient times, and they have contemporary meaning and purpose.

In early times, oblations were offered into fire. Herbs and clarified butter were poured into a fire while *mantras* and scriptures were chanted to purify the atmosphere. These holy sounds honored the divine powers in the form of the primordial elements. The vibrations of divine energy purified a person's internal and external environment and the atmosphere. Sound is the property of space; sound waves move through space. Our thoughts and speech directly affect our atmosphere. When we sit calmly and quietly in meditation and recite our mantra, this holy vibration impacts the space around us and within us. When our speech is constructive and honest, we enhance our environment. When we gossip and speak in hurtful ways, we pollute the space we inhabit. Telling lies and misleading others is sinful, while speaking truth is virtuous.

We should remember and appreciate the sacrifice of those who have come before us. Many people have offered their energy and abilities to uplift society. We benefit from their sacrifices and the wealth of knowledge they passed on. Taking their gifts for granted is a form of stealing, while acknowledging them with gratitude nourishes our learning environment.

Welcoming guests uplifts society, and helping those who are suffering and in need strengthens us all. Opening our homes and our lives to others has a transformative effect in our neighborhoods and throughout society. Offering our ability to care for any suffering being generates an atmosphere of healing.

We must not overlook the countless ways animals, birds, insects, trees and plants help the earth. At one time, farmers added only animal waste to the earth to enrich the soil before plowing. Animal waste from vegetarian animals is medicine for the soil. Offering this manure to the land before plowing and cultivating the field was helpful for the earth, plant life, animals and humankind. Using this fertilizer, farmers respected the land and cared for the environment. Now chemicals are used to enhance production out of greed for increased profits. Toxic fertilizers cause disease in humanity; harm or kill helpful organisms, insects and animals; and pollute the land and water. We are able to make many choices every day that help to sustain and support the earth and our environment, including recycling, supporting organic farmers and conserving energy.

Every person lives indebted to the five primordial elements. We free ourselves of this debt by revitalizing these ancient sacrificial practices in our daily lives. Our life is based in the divine elements. Earth, water, fire, air, and space are divine powers and they are unlimited. We should not think that earth refers only to this small planet on which we live. This is one example of the element of earth. There are numerous planets in this cosmos related with millions of stars, each with their own family of planets. The earth element is immeasurable, just as all the elements are infinite, and whatever is infinite is divine. In meditation we can visualize sitting on this small globe moving through endless space. There are millions of globes sharing the same divine space and each one is a projection of divine energy in the form of earth. At the ocean, we see many waves coming onto shore and merging back into the ocean. In the same way, countless nebulas, galaxies and stars are appearing in this ocean of energy and merging back into divine energy. It is impossible to know about all of this. It is beyond our perception and reach. It is limitless.

Wherever we are in this divine expression, we have a duty to participate. We should perform our duty, helping to purify and honor our atmosphere with holy behavior. This is called *yagya*. When we develop our awareness of and gratitude to the divine powers, then these divine powers provide for us. If we cherish them, we benefit from their support and nourishment. Every action causes a reaction. What we give to this environment returns to us with equal power.

This universe is called *brahmananda*, a golden, cosmic egg. We live within this atmosphere. When we emit a sound; we also hear the sound we made. Whatever sound we send forth returns to our ears. It is a divine law that we receive back the echo of our vibration. In the same way everything we do brings results back to us. When we work to value and care for our environment the divine powers automatically nurture our efforts.

God is one, infinite supreme source. But as we have different limbs and each limb has different functions and abilities, the manifestation of one supreme being has many limbs and faculties. Each one is a divine power with its own unique quality and purpose. The divine powers are the faculties of one cosmic being. When we worship this cosmic expression, all divine powers are cherished by our feelings of devotion and love, our trust and our deeds. When we value and honor the divine powers, automatically they nourish and support us. In this process we move toward the highest good.

Our lives depend on these divine powers and we are able to give to others because of what we receive from divinity. We claim ownership of our abilities and faculties because we think they are in our possession, but we do not create, nor do we own these elements. Whatever was, is, and will be is a manifestation of the supreme source. In this way, all life belongs to divine power; our part in this divine expression is very small. When we realize that all belongs to divinity and has existed from time immemorial, we develop gratitude for all that makes our small existence and our actions possible.

Our knowledge, vigor, and body are gifts from Godhead. Our ego is the only thing that belongs to us. All of our cognitive and active senses were not created by us, but given to us. The primordial elements that constitute our body are part and parcel of the divine elements. Our ego and our pride alone are ours to claim. We have a small place in this manifestation and we use the divine faculties to function. We could not exist without these divine gifts.

In chapter XVIII, Krishna tells us that there are five parts to our action and we can only claim one: ego.[55] Our ego is one and the other four are divine powers. Divine powers help us, and our capabilities are the result of this combined effort, not our effort alone. If we think we are the doer, and the results of our action belong to us, we are stealing the results from the other participants in our action.[56] We are thieves, taking and hoarding what rightfully belongs to others.

---

[55] *Bhagavad Gītā* XVIII/13-15.
[56] *Bhagavad Gītā* III/12.

According to divine law, four partners always assist the work of our ego: the body, means, knowledge and protection. The basis of action is the body itself. This is our most important partner. Without a body we cannot act. The body, the seat of action, is made up of the five primordial elements. Unfortunately, we overlook the divine powers that provide us with a body. The divine powers are the means for enlivening our cognitive and active senses. Knowledge also supports us; work is possible because we have a base of knowledge and the capacity to make or gather the tools necessary for our work. And protection is a vital participant in any endeavor; it is important to work safely.

All the elements and factors that give us a body, the means, knowledge and protection for our action share in the results of our action. Countless people and divine qualities assist us. We take credit for our accomplishments and the money we make, but we did not create our knowledge and resources. Each of us receives knowledge from many sources to develop our skills and abilities. It is impossible to identify all the people who directly or indirectly aided the development of our knowledge, worked to preserve knowledge in books, and helped us gain our position in society. These are all partners in our activity.

Every person and power assisting us participates with our doer and is entitled to a share in the results of our action. We should maintain an attitude of gratitude to the countless participants supporting our action, rather than think we are solely responsible for the benefits of our action. In this way we do not steal the share of others. Nowadays, we are taxed, and must give a share of our earnings to help with education, research, and the protection of our government. We may think we are supporting others, but really we are giving a share to those who support us.

We must become aware of the source of our life and the forces and people helping us to live and act. By honoring them, we increase our nourishment and decrease our suffering. A sacrificial attitude is necessary for peace and happiness. This universe is maintained through sacrifice, and only through sacrifice can society be maintained. We were born due to the sacrifice of our mother and father, and we are raised by teachers and countless others. We are committing a great sin if we do not continue in this process of sacrifice, and we will suffer the consequences of our harmful behavior. We must develop gratitude for the powers and people supporting our lives.

September 1, 1998

III/12 When we work on behalf of this universal being, then all divine faculties and deities are cherished and they bless us. But if we act against this divine process, taking these gifts for granted and failing to offer sacrifice to the divine powers in return, we are stealing.

III/13 The good, who eat the remainder of sacrifice, are released from all evils. The wicked, who cook only for their own sake, eat their own impurity.

We are part and parcel of this universe, this body of cosmic *purusha* or cosmic being. As we each have a body, this universe is the body of cosmic being. This cosmic being comes into existence when unmanifest nature is inspired by spirit; divine energy and pure consciousness join together.[57] Pure consciousness and all-pervasive energy are both eternal and infinite. They are the cause of this cosmic being, and numerous other universes as well. The supreme cause of all universes is one: *Brahman*. *Brahman* or Godhead is infinite knowledge and bliss, the supreme source of eternal nature and consciousness.

In Sanskrit, *brahmā* is the name for cosmic being and the body of the universe is called *brahmananda*. In English, the level of existence called *brahmā* would be called God. Each *brahmā* is the creator of a *brahmananda*, or universe, and every universe has its own soul. There is one *brahmā*

---

[57] Krishna refers to supreme spirit as *aksaram Brahman* (VIII/3) and supreme nature as *mahad brahma* (XIV/3).

or God in each universe. Every human life is part and parcel of this universal cosmic being. We cannot breathe or function without the grace of this divine being.

Philosophically, when we refer to God as our father, we are referring to this cosmic being. Our body, mind, senses, strength, ability, intellect, everything we have exists by the grace of *brahmā*. Our action on behalf of this cosmic being is called sacrifice, *yagya*. "When we work on behalf of this universal being, then all divine faculties and deities are cherished and they bless us. But if we act against this divine process, taking these gifts for granted and failing to offer sacrifice to the divine powers in return, we are stealing."[58]

When we act against divine will and take without offering our work as a sacrifice, then we do not receive divine grace. Without divine grace, we suffer. This is the root of suffering: we ignore divine power and do not offer our abilities and gifts for the benefit of this universe, but take and use these gifts to seek our own wealth and pleasure. When we behave like this, we deprive ourselves of divine grace. We steal and hoard gifts that do not belong to us, and we forfeit divine blessings.

We cannot perform action without impacting society. We may think our action only relates to us, but every action affects our environment. Eating, drinking, talking, moving, everything we do has an environmental impact and influences society. We must realize how profoundly our environment and community support us, and choose our behavior carefully. According to Vedic thought, we have three kinds of debt. We are indebted to our family

---

[58] *Bhagavad Gītā* III/12.

and ancestors, to the seers and teachers who have worked to preserve and share knowledge, and to the divine powers.

Our mothers and fathers were each raised in their own families and social circumstances where many people provided knowledge and service. They were nourished, protected, and taught by countless people, including all of the people who came before to establish their communities and support the people in their lives. This lineage from each parent is called *pitri*. Our individual development and nourishment comes directly from our parents and indirectly from their ancestry. We are indebted to our parents and forebears.

The second debt is to our teachers. The knowledge I am presenting is not my own knowledge. I received this knowledge through a spiritual lineage of teachers. My teacher, his teacher, and all teachers of this knowledge share the same source: the divine power in the form of cosmic being is the teacher of all. Supreme truth has come through a long line of seers and teachers. We are indebted to them and to the knowledge they share. This knowledge offers methods for developing skills and abilities that lead to upliftment.

Finally, we are indebted to the divine powers. Without the sun, moon, earth, water, fire, air, space and other deities, we would not exist and could not function in any way. We owe our lives and our capacity for action to the divine faculties.

All of these contributors sacrificed for us. Our debt can only be paid through honoring them and continuing the process of sacrifice. There is no other way. Krishna tells us that when we cherish divine power with our sacrifices, the process continues and we are blessed. If we take without giving back, we are stealing from the divine powers and all who have sacrificed for our welfare and the welfare of humankind. We also rob ourselves, because we do not experience the nourishment and support we receive when our lives are aligned with this eternal process. We may be able to avoid our debtors, but we cannot hide from divinity. If we do not participate in this process, we lose our connection to divine grace and we suffer.

Krishna urges us to live a divine life as a saint. "The good, who eat the remainder of sacrifice, are released from all evils." [59] Our duty is to perform action to the best of our abilities, inspired by sacrifice. After offering our work as a sacrifice, Krishna instructs us to eat the remnants of sacrifice. In other words, we should be satisfied by the gifts bestowed as a result of our action. Without expectations, we enjoy the blessings of divinity. We are content and avoid the evils of expectation, craving, wanting specific results, and suffering from comparisons, disappointment and loss.

No matter what our profession, whether we are a householder or a renunciant, we can practice *yagya*. Any businessperson, laborer, teacher or renunciant can live as a saint. Sainthood is not limited to people who have left the activities of the world. A saint is a person who becomes free from evil – a person with pure thought and action. Saints act with their minds and hearts free from desire and pollution. Purity is gained when we enjoy the remnant of sacrifice. We offer our hearts and minds in service of

---

[59] *Bhagavad Gītā* III/13.

divinity, and what remains with us is our share. In this way, we are freed from sins and vices and we enjoy divine grace.

Sainthood is not accomplished by donning a special cloth or placing a mark on the forehead. Thoughts, behavior, and deeds make us saintly. When our behavior is sacrificial and we are satisfied with the remnant, our contentment indicates sainthood. Great saints and *yogis* perform action with detachment, knowing attachment is the root cause of bondage. They are free from expectation, but not from action. With a pure heart and mind, they perform their work as a sacrifice, enjoying purity of heart and peace of mind.

There was once a weaver who was a saint. The king invited him to his palace, where the princess saw her father prostrate before him. She decided that he would be her husband. She told her father and the saint came forward to speak with her.

"I am a simple man living in a hut near the jungle. I have no luxuries," he explained. "I would not be able to accept any palace offered by your father or brothers."

She replied that she wanted him as her husband and that was all. They were married and the princess lived with him in his hut. Every day she prepared wool and he weaved cloth. In the evening he would go to the market, sell the cloth, and buy some food. When he returned, she would prepare a simple meal. This was their daily routine. The saint would not take donations from anyone, but worked by his own hand to earn money for food. The rest of the day was spent in study and meditation.

One day, when the saint went to the market, some devious men decided to test him. They heard that the saint had conquered the six great enemies: delusion, lust, anger, greed, pride, and egoism. To challenge him, they asked to inspect the cloth he had weaved that day. One of the men tore it in half and asked, "Now, what is your cloth worth?"

The saint replied, "One-half rupee for each half."

Again the man tore each piece in half, and laughed at the saint saying, "What do you think these are worth?"

The saint replied, "One-quarter rupee each."

The man then threw the cloth on the ground and said, "Who will buy these now? They are useless."

The saint smiled, picked up his cloth and returned home.

Another man decided to test the saint further. He followed him home, thinking he would try to fondle his wife.

When the saint arrived home, his wife looked for the food he normally brought after selling the cloth. His hands were empty. "God suggested that we fast today," the saintly weaver told her.

Suddenly, the man who had followed him stepped forward, grabbed the wife and ran, pulling her with him. The saint watched calmly and then, using divine powers, gave the man a blow to his head. The man went unconscious. Then the saint told his wife to bring herbs and clarified butter, which he used to nurse the man back to consciousness.

When the man awoke, he mocked the saint saying, "I was successful in making you angry."

The saint laughed and said, "O my boy, if I were angry I would not have nursed you back to life. When you created trouble for my food I could adjust. But when you touched my wife, I knew that your passion and lust would return to you over and again, creating much trouble for her. I had to check your bad habit."

We can adjust to the discomforts others may cause us, but if a person creates real trouble in our life, we must interrupt their behavior and try to shed light on their harmful actions. This is not giving into anger but aligning with divine law. A saintly life is not related with our position in society. A saint may live in any condition or circumstance, but lives with a pure mind, heart, and deeds.

We make ourselves pure by simply enjoying the remnants of our action. We offer what we have to divinity, acknowledge all who contribute to our capabilities, are content with the results we receive, and do not covet more. We each have a head, a heart, and hands. The action of our hands begins in our head and heart; what we do is a projection of our thoughts and feelings. We need both knowledge and will to perform sacrificial work. Without knowledge we cannot act wisely, and without determination we lack motivation. We need purity in our thoughts and feelings for our behavior and deeds to be beneficial and without bondage.

Krishna warns, "The wicked, who cook only for their own sake, eat their own impurity."[60] A sinful life is full of vices. It is the abode of delusion, lust, anger, greed, pride, and egoism. Sinful people act only for their own enjoyment and pleasure. They think of their own benefit without regard to others. Thinking always, "I must enjoy, I must have," their motives are selfish. Selfish motivation is the root cause of sin. These people disregard society, including divinity, teachers, and ancestors. They ignore the

---

[60] *Bhagavad Gītā* III/13.

ones who provide for us all. Their effort is only for their own enjoyment, to satisfy their own passions. Egoistic and prideful, they sin and bring suffering into their lives.

We are all members of one divine family. In the eyes of divinity, all children have the same position, and are blessed equally with love, grace, and affection. Regardless of our ability or state of development we are all vessels of divine love. Whether we collect garbage or teach in a university, we all have the same value to Godhead and we can work on behalf of our divine family in service to Godhead. When we perform our work with a sacrificial motive, we enjoy divine grace. But if we work only for selfish motives, we suffer. Our motivation is what matters, not our position in society. Divine grace and love are the same for the laborer, the merchant, the teacher, or the renunciant.

September 2, 1998

III/14 Our life comes into existence from food. Food results from rain; rain from sacrifice; and sacrifice is made possible by action.

III/15 Know that the origin of action is *Brahman*. All of this nature arises from imperishable being. Therefore, the all-pervading *Brahman* is eternally established in sacrifice.

The main principle behind *karma yoga* is that no one lives without action. Our present situation is the result of our past action; and what we do now creates our future. To free ourselves from suffering, we relate our actions with our supreme cause. We need to realize we are a projection of infinity; part and parcel of this cosmic being. Our body is a projection of divine energy and our soul is a manifestation of supreme consciousness. Without this cosmic being – the source of our life – we could not draw a single breath. When we realize every action we take is related with our supreme cause, our lives align with divinity and our actions serve divinity. This is called *karma yoga* and practitioners are called *karma yogis*.

When our actions are consciously chosen on behalf of divinity, we are worshipping God. Our work is holy and we feel whole. But when our minds pull us toward identification with the physical and sensual world of diversity, we think we are this limited body, separate and lacking. We feel incomplete and we try to satisfy ourselves through the senses and body. We live in anxiety, moving hither and thither between pleasure and pain. This is *karma bhoga*. In truth, we are all *karma yogis* because our actions cannot be disconnected from our supreme source, but when we are unaware of this reality, our ignorance causes uncertainty and misery.

When we understand that we are an aspect of divinity and are instruments of divinity, we enjoy bliss and feel emancipation. Our every action is on behalf of Godhead and is *yagya* or sacrifice. We feel our connection to infinity and we are free of insecurity. This is the antidote to human suffering, which is caused by selfish actions. When our motivation for action is the desire to fulfill our limited mental and sensual demands, we suffer and are bound by our actions. Our mind and our senses are limited, and our efforts to satisfy their demands trap us in limitation. Everyone has a body and a soul. Acting on behalf of our whole being leads to emancipation, while acting on behalf of our body alone is the cause of bondage. This is a simple teaching.

We should be inspired by divinity and use our abilities and capabilities, focusing our full attention on appropriate, skillful action. Whatever we gain from our effort is the remnant of our sacrifice. We accept this as a blessing from divinity. This process keeps our hearts and minds pure, free from the cravings that lead to wrongdoing. When cravings lead us into action, we are never satisfied and we suffer. Virtue and sacrifice lead us to lasting happiness because *yagya* is the cause and continuity of life.

"Our life comes into existence from food. Food results from rain; rain from sacrifice; and sacrifice is made possible by action."[61] Food nourishes our existence. The

---

[61] *Bhagavad Gītā* III/14.

food we eat changes into three forms. One form is nutrients; the other two forms are liquid and solid wastes. The nutrients enter our bloodstream to nourish our tissues and to make fat and bone. The gist of bone is marrow, and marrow produces semen.[62] Semen carries sperm to an egg, and together sperm and egg form an embryo. Our mortal body – the abode of the soul – is the result of this process, which begins with food. Therefore, our food needs to be pure in order to create sacred life energy and healthy children. Food is not possible without rain. Rain water is essential for our vegetables, fruits, and grains. A divine sacrificial process causes the rain that helps produce our food. The sun gives heat, which lifts water from the ocean, creating clouds of moisture, and the clouds release rain. This process of giving and receiving is *yagya*. *Yagya* is the root cause of existence and actions. Every aspect of our lives and our environment evolve from sacrifice.

Without the sun, there would be no life on earth. We are all indebted to the sun's sacrificial activity, which makes life possible. The sun is the manifestation of the supreme cause, and the sun's existence is inspired by sacrifice. Godhead offers pure knowledge into nature, inspiring the movement of divine energy. The increasing movement of divine energy creates light and heat, forming a golden egg. The continued friction of nature projects into this universe. All action and life originate from the initial sacrifice of our supreme cause. The sun is the manifested form of Godhead and the abode of pure knowledge. We can see the form of the sun, but not the true reality of the sun. We all have a soul within us. Others

---

[62] This is a traditional sequence of the transformation of human life, from food to reproduction.

see our physical body, but cannot see our soul or true self. In the same way, we see the sun's form or body, while the soul of the sun resides invisible within that form.

Everything existing in form has a soul. The natural elements of energy are constantly in motion and would never take shape without a magnetic force. Forms are made when diverse elements are held together by an attractive power. This attractive power is called soul. It is impossible for the diverse elements of nature to join together and take shape without a magnetic center or nucleus. Our physical body exists because our subtle body – our soul – attracts and holds various elements in one form. When our subtle body departs, these elements disperse and our body decays. Our form takes shape because the soul resides in our body.

Every form depends on an attractive power, and our ancient seers declared that each tree, plant, and living creature has its own soul. Everything that grows, feels, and reproduces carries a soul. The form can be seen, the soul cannot. What we see with our eyes and call the sun is the body of the sun. Residing in that body is pure consciousness and knowledge, the soul of this universe. The divine sun is the root cause of this universe. The soul of the sun is pure knowledge. We each carry this soul within us because the sun is the source of our life. Every particle and action in our universe originates from this abode of pure knowledge.

When we connect our actions with pure consciousness and knowledge, we are performing *yagya*. "Know that the origin of action is *Brahman*. All of this nature arises from imperishable being. Therefore, the all-pervading *Brahman* is eternally established in sacrifice."[63] *Brahman* is infinite knowledge. All action originates from *Brahman*. Without knowledge or the inspiration of pure consciousness, nothing exists and no action is possible. The knowledge of the soul is the base of sacrificial action.

In order to perform sacrificial action, we need a body and we need the inspiration of the soul. These are the two facets of human life. Our mortal body is related with the projection of divine energy and our immortal soul is the manifestation of pure knowledge and consciousness. Knowledge is the property of Godhead. It is infinite, eternal, and imperishable. Whatever knowledge we have is a projection of divinity. Our knowledge is bestowed by divinity and our soul is a manifestation of pure knowledge. We are always connected with our source of knowledge; we are always one with the source of our life. Our seers tell us that the soul of the sun is the abode of knowledge and life, the father of our individual soul. Our individual soul is a ray of light from the sun. All action takes place in the physical world, but it is always generated by knowledge, the property of the soul. Therefore knowledge is the heart of *yagya*, sacrificial action.

We never act unless inspired. We may be inspired by pure knowledge or prompted by the desire for objects. Knowledge resides in sacrificial action, not in sensual desire. When our action is inspired by knowledge, it is *yagya*. When we perform yagya, we allow knowledge to enliven truth, and we act with devotion. Knowledge is not limited in the way forms of nature are limited. It is an all-pervasive power. It is not constructed of bundles of

---

[63] *Bhagavad Gītā* III/15.

energy; it is the observer of energy. Knowledge exists above and beyond energy, yet it manifests and works through energy in the form of our intellect. Knowledge remains infinite while infusing all energy and action. Knowledge is established throughout energy's sacrificial movement.

Sacrifice is action in the light of divine knowledge. It is not a special kind of ritual or service. Any action is an offering when it is done in the light of divine knowledge. We must be aware that what we do affects our own lives, our community, our environment, and the divine process of all existence. Sacrifice begins with *Brahman's* inspiration and continues at all levels of this universe. When we act in the light of knowledge, we worship divinity and live with divine grace.

Putting *Karma Yoga* into Practice
July 24, 1997
Self-Cultivation

Just as a farmer must tend to every aspect of plant growth in order to harvest a healthy crop, we need to cultivate ourselves so that we may experience ultimate truth and bliss. Cultivation is the work of removing anything undesirable from our lives, while adding and developing enriching practices. We remove our misconceptions about our separate identity and cultivate knowledge and awareness of our unity with supreme being. The great seers taught that practice is necessary to purify our intellects and minds, allowing this realization to dawn within us. Again and again, we think about our source of life and our minds gradually align with the qualities of spirit, allowing an awareness of ultimate truth to develop within us. This is the process of cultivation. We cultivate our hearts, minds, and intellects, steadily dwelling on the source of intelligence and blissfulness. "The person who is not one with the supreme cause is without wisdom and concentration. This person's heart is impure. Without a pure heart there is no peace. And without peace there is no happiness."[64]

We all share the same source of life and receive life energy from this one source. Life energy is divine because it is indivisible. We cannot divide the earth. We can draw a line and superimpose a division, arguing that there is a

---

[64] *Bhagavad Gītā* II/66.

difference between the two sides, but we cannot truly portion out the earth. Likewise, we cannot divide water, fire, air, or space. These are divine elements and divinity cannot be divided. Divinity belongs to all beings and every being has the right to use what is divine. Everything we see in visual or perceptible form is a projection of the same ultimate truth. We give many names to this truth, but truth is one, absolute infinity. It cannot be divided.

We are all given tools for cultivation. These tools are projections of nature. Our instruments include intellect, ego, mind, the five cognitive senses, the five active senses, and the primordial elements,[65] which form the gross body. We all have these same instruments; we share the same potential. We can use our tools to chase pleasure or to develop refinement. Our instruments are useless by themselves because they are part of nature and nature is insentient. Insentient nature is not capable of doing anything without the enlivening consciousness of spirit.

Spirit is sentient and works through the means provided by nature. Patanjali explains that nature has three attributes: *sattoguna* or light, *rajoguna* or movement, and *tamoguna* or stability. These three qualities project into all the elements and instruments. These materials allow us to come into a human form, engage in experience, and seek emancipation.[66] Patanjali also teaches that all of nature exists for that seer (spirit).[67] Nature provides the means for spirit to manifest and become known. It is the means for our learning and development.

---

[65] The primordial elements are space, air, fire, water, and earth.
[66] *Yoga Sūtras* II/18.
[67] *Yoga Sūtras* II/21.

Intellect is the greatest tool provided by divinity. The intellect develops through a long process of evolution, and only fully developed beings – human beings – are able to use this unique gift of divine energy. Our ability to use the intellect to reason is a defining quality of being human. Our *brahma chakra*, the energy center at the top of the head, is the place of intellect. When the *brahma chakra* receives the light of spirit, our intellect becomes conscious and is able to reason and discriminate. This initial inspiration enlivens the intellect and produces a sense of existence or consciousness called soul.

The intellect's ability to be enlivened by consciousness is comparable to the way an iron ball captures the qualities of light and heat when placed in a fire. Light and heat are the properties of fire, but when iron is placed in fire, it begins to receive and adopt the properties of fire. After some time, the ball of iron appears to be a ball of fire because the iron has taken on the fire's light and heat. Iron has this capacity. In the same way, our intellect is able to receive and adopt the qualities of spirit: knowledge, truth, and infinity. Other words used for these qualities are intelligence, existence, and bliss. Because the intellect receives and adopts the qualities of spirit, it is a medium for the manifestation of spirit.

The soul – our pure sense of existence that comes from the initial enlivening of the intellect – is called *aham* in Sanskrit, which means "I-am." When I-am accepts the form or limitation of the medium as its own shape, then it loses its purity and is called *ahamkara*. *Aham* means ego or center of existence, while *ahamkara* indicates the limitations of the ego. When the sense of existence takes ownership of its finite form, thinking "this is mine," then ego becomes egoism or *ahamkara*. Patanjali states, "To accept the non-eternal, the impure, the cause of suffering, and the non-self as eternal, pure, the abode of happiness, and the real self is *avidya*, nescience or ignorance."[68] This misidentification is the root cause of suffering[69] and it produces *asmita*, egoism.[70] Individuality is experienced because the medium is individual, and we fail to realize that the source of consciousness enlivening every single medium is one supreme truth.

Supreme spirit is one infinite absolute. People use different names, such as *Brahman* or Godhead, for this absolute; but truly it is beyond all names and forms. The world of nature, where all names and forms exist, is the medium through which supreme spirit manifests. Our individual soul is a manifestation of cosmic being. When we reach a higher level of consciousness, we realize that all diversity is a projection of one ultimate truth. One unity projects throughout this diverse universe and it is not possible for any part of this whole diversity to exist separate from unity. When we realize our oneness with supreme being, we feel oneness with all beings. We see the same self residing in all and love for all beings grows within us.

Our intellects have collected countless impressions over time. Many are false and useless. Our undesirable patterns of thinking lead us away from our real self and cause us suffering. When we begin to seek the realization of unity, our wrong impressions jump in front of us. They are most obvious when we sit in meditation. It can be

---

[68] *Yoga Sūtras* II/5.
[69] *Yoga Sūtras* II/4.
[70] *Yoga Sūtras* II/6.

overwhelming to experience the impact of our thoughts in meditation. Our undesirable impressions appear against our will. These latent impressions arise as we train our minds to be calm and quiet. We should not be afraid or discouraged. As we continue our practice, we are able to consistently remove these undesirable tendencies. In meditation, we can counter the power of these impressions by visualizing endless space. We turn our attention to what is whole and undivided, and these limiting impressions lose their power. Gradually, with determined effort, we release them and they dissolve. Persistence is needed to make change in our lives. With perseverance and practice, all undesirable obstacles can be removed and we can become free.

Undesirable patterns of thinking are projections of *rajoguna*. When one attribute of nature is dominant in us, our behavior reflects that quality. *Sattoguna* is light, and *sattvic* thoughts and actions are pure and uplifting. *Tamoguna* is dense delusion and ignorance, and *tamasic* impressions and behavior are corrupt and destructive. When *tamoguna* dominates, meditation is almost impossible. *Rajoguna* is movement, desire and passion, and *rajasic* tendencies are indiscriminate and unstable. We need to channel the movement of *rajoguna* towards divine service and draw it away from our desires and passions. This is the purpose behind *karma yoga*. Divine service provides an expression for our *rajasic* movement, and our actions are purified when guided by *sattoguna* or knowledge.

Everyone has three means for action: thought, speech, and body. Our minds are engaged in all of our behavior, our speech has a powerful impact, and our bodies are capable of countless actions. We need to cultivate ourselves, seeking a way to think, speak and act on behalf of divinity. When we relate our thoughts, speech, and actions with divinity, we serve divinity. We perform good and dutiful work. There is no need to leave society; we simply function within our situation, focused on divinity rather than the fruits of our actions. This checks our behavior and keeps our hearts, minds, and intellects pure. Accordingly, we develop impressions that lead us towards unity.

We should eliminate actions driven by selfish motives and avoid undesirable behavior that hinders our divine path. Wrong impressions fuel our cravings because we feed them. When we become aware of our selfish motives, we can use our discrimination and determination to remove them. Gradually they do not return to disturb our peace. In time, we develop and nourish healthy impressions that support us along our divine path.

Intellect gives us the ability to choose. We can choose and cultivate good tendencies. In agriculture, a farmer plows the land, removes undesirable objects, adds nourishment to the soil, and then sows seeds. In a similar manner, we cultivate our intellects, hearts and actions. We dig into the soil of ourselves; weeding out negative thoughts, words and behaviors; enriching ourselves with inspiring texts, teachers and meditation; planting the seeds of useful thoughts and actions; and nurturing and protecting what we have planted. In time, we receive a bounty.

As we work to cultivate ourselves, our thoughts are the plow. Read and contemplate divine knowledge; listen to the wise and think upon their words. These sources offer guidance as we work to purify the intellect. Cultivating the intellect with knowledge helps us choose what is useful and reject what is destructive. Scriptures and good company encourage impressions that clarify our thoughts, speech and actions.

Higher knowledge and divine teachings inspire us to create change and remove the impressions that limit us and cause suffering. They light the way and support us as we seek appropriate choices for a divine path. Good qualities and uplifting tendencies take root when we cultivate our understanding of the source and purpose of our lives.

July 25, 1997
Practical Knowledge

Our existence is a state of consciousness. Our physical body is like a garment we wear. Consciousness is infinite, unlimited and all-pervasive. The properties of consciousness are intelligence, existence and bliss. We are able to inhabit human existence and experience the qualities of consciousness when these qualities are expressed through a medium of nature. This medium for expression is able to receive and adopt the qualities and properties of supreme spirit.

The divine power of Godhead is called nature or energy, and this energy is the source of all manifested forms. Energy is limitless, weightless, colorless, formless, and infinite. In physics we find the same idea: bundles of energy transform into and out of form. Energy is neither created nor destroyed during this process; it only appears in forms and disappears into formlessness. When energy compounds into forms, we are able to perceive the effects of energy, but when the effects return to their source in unmanifest energy, then energy is no longer perceptible.

In *Vedānta* philosophy, energy is called *māyā* and in *Sāmkhya* philosophy it is called *prakriti*. Although various traditions give the power of energy many different names, energy is beyond description. *Māyā* is just one way to indicate the divine power of Godhead. This power enables the indescribable to become describable. In Sanskrit, *mā* means "measure" and *yā* means "who." *Māyā* is the divine power, which provides the means for immeasurable infinity to be expressed in measurable forms. In other words, *māyā* limits the immeasurable into forms that can be seen and understood. As electricity is an unlimited, unseen power that requires the limitations of a bulb to be seen as light, supreme consciousness – existence, intelligence, and bliss – can only be experienced when expressing through a medium or form.

In *Yoga*, the first projection or form of nature is called *chitta*. This is referred to as the *brahma chakra* in the *Upanishads*, and *mahat* in *Sāmkhya*. This first modification of nature is the limited container for the infinite qualities of intelligence, existence, and bliss. When these qualities are contained, they can be realized by an individual. Once this medium is enlivened by consciousness the individual intellect forms. Our intellect has the ability to adopt and reflect whatever we hold close: the light of consciousness or the darkness of our desire for objects.

The light of supreme spirit enlivens this medium of nature, causing movement and making it possible for us to experience life. Spirit is pure knowledge or intelligence, while movement is the property of existence. Godhead initiates movement by offering inspiring spirit into the energy of nature. This sacrifice is divine love or bliss. When we realize our intelligence and existence are manifestations of supreme spirit, we experience oneness. Our unity with Godhead is a profound state of blissful love.

Unfortunately, in our journey through lifetimes, we mistake the qualities of unlimited consciousness as our own individual qualities. This false belief leads to our feelings of separation from Godhead. Our self-imposed loss of unity with Godhead is the root of misguided thinking. Our misunderstanding makes us feel isolated and hollow, and our attempt to fill our sense of emptiness with material nature creates many destructive tendencies and wrong impressions. Life vibrates with our yearning to reunite with the eternal divine bliss and unity we first experienced when supreme spirit enlivened our individual medium. This initial oneness engenders our constant quest to return to bliss and discover our source.

Our external search to fulfill this inner demand causes restlessness and sadness. It is a heart-breaking misunderstanding; we are never separate from Godhead. Practice is directed at clarifying this misunderstanding and practice requires effort. Again and again, we must seek the truth: we will never experience bliss or love by uniting with objects in the external world. Gradually, we replace our false impressions with the realization of our eternal, everlasting union with our source in consciousness. This union, called *yoga*, exists within our real self. Our practice is the cultivation of this realization.

When we relate our life energy, abilities, and intelligence with Godhead, performing our duties and responsibilities on behalf of Godhead, this is *karma yoga*. We focus on unity, not on the fruits of this diverse world. We accept the remnants we receive from our actions as divine grace from Godhead. We purify our intellects, minds, and hearts by acting without desire, greed, or pride.

When we realize unity in diversity, we attain ultimate truth. This is the purpose of human life. We cultivate ourselves until we are able to see the same self appearing in all beings. We realize there is no division, separation, limitation or barrier. With our understanding of unity comes love and respect for all. This is a divine experience.

This truth is beyond our vision and perception. Our eyes see what is outside, but cannot see ultimate truth. When we awaken in the morning and see the sun rising, it looks like a small, beautiful ball that rises through the sky around our earth. We have seen this happen repeatedly throughout our lives. But how does reality compare to what we see? The sun is many times larger than our earth, and our earth is moving around the sun. We cannot look through our eyes to see the truth. We find the truth through our intellect, not our eyes. Our eyes look out on this diverse world, but our intellect is able to see reality and envision the unity behind this diversity.

Our intellect is near to ultimate truth. Our intellect receives the qualities of supreme spirit and becomes conscious when adopting these qualities. Our sense of existence, I-amness, awakens when our intellect is enlivened by supreme spirit. Our soul or true self is the experience of intelligence and existence, the properties of spirit, manifesting in our intellect. When we realize we are part and parcel of Godhead, we experience the divine blissful love of unity with our source.

July 28, 1997
Devotion

According to my realization, the source of life is our goal in life. We should try to understand this aim and realize that our inner demand can only be satisfied with the experience of infinite, supreme consciousness. Our lives originate in infinity and when we realize we are inseparable from this divine source we attain ultimate truth. We all want to be free from ignorance, the feeling of emptiness, and the fear of death. These are the main causes of suffering. We seek intelligence, eternal existence, and infinite happiness, and these are the qualities of supreme consciousness.

Our soul is part and parcel of supreme consciousness, and is above the movement of nature. And yet nature's movement is essential in our search to experience supreme consciousness. We cannot survive a single moment without action. "All humans should wish to live for one hundred years continuously performing action. Without action, one's life is useless; without purpose, or value."[71] We will never reach the aim of life or experience true bliss without performing action. We must choose our action wisely. When action is rooted in desire, it binds the soul. A powerful chain of bondage is created when our love turns into desire and our actions are focused on fulfilling desire. Life is a manifestation of divine light, which we experience as bliss or love. When we project our love out toward the

---

[71] *Īsa Upanishad* 2.

things of this world, love becomes desire. Desire motivates actions, which bring the results of enjoyment and lead to attachment; these are the links in a chain that binds us to the cycle of birth and death. We can only break free of this chain by realizing that our true self is one with the source of intelligence, existence and bliss. Our love is fulfilled when we turn inside towards our source. By understanding our real position, we are freed from the cycle of bondage.

Light, life and love are all related. These qualities are eternal; they project from one infinite supreme spirit. Divine light manifests in our *brahma chakra*, enlivening us, and we experience this light as pure love. This experience is eternal. Light, life and love are infinite and beyond the changes of nature. In our lives, love exists as affection for children, respect for our parents, or companionship with a spouse. Love inspires the wish that all beings find their connection with the source of life. Love can take many forms.

When our love becomes attached with worldly objects, it loses its purity and degrades into desire. Love related with sex becomes passion or lust. Love for wealth becomes greed. With any hindrance, love becomes anger. If we are threatened, we fear losing what we love. When love is expressed as desire, it can turn into addiction. All emotions are variations of one life energy called love.

Love can gaze outward or focus on the source of our lives. When love faces toward the external world it becomes emotion, and when it turns toward the source of life, it is devotion. This is an important distinction because our actions will either be driven by our emotions or inspired by devotion. As we come to understand that emotion is an outward manifestation of divine love, we can gradually free ourselves from the bondage of desire. Love is not for worldly objects, passion or lust; it is for devotion. Pure love is the experience of our connection with divinity. We can devote ourselves to any form or concept of divinity, but our devotion must be one-pointed.[72] We cannot be with this today and with that tomorrow. Love is not fickle, but steadfast. By making our love one-pointed, our agitated mind becomes stable and our stable mind becomes pure. With a pure mind, it is possible to realize the supreme cause. With realization, devotion fills our hearts.

At first, there is no need to focus on the supreme being. It is difficult to focus on something unknown to us. We begin by putting our mind on what is near and dear to us. Gradually this one-pointed practice leads us to the source of our life. In order to reach the experience of infinite bliss, we must practice with a steady, focused effort.

There is a wonderful story about a farmer who approaches his guru with the desire to learn meditation and realize the supreme Lord. The guru explains to the farmer that he should spend some time alone and fix his mind on whatever is dear to him. The guru offers a room at his ashram where the farmer's needs will be cared for while he devotes time to meditation.

The guru suggests that the farmer set aside fifty days for this process to take root. He instructs him to live in one room and concentrate only on what is dear to him. The farmer has a beautiful bull that he loves very much.

---

[72] *Yoga Sūtras* I/23, 28, 29, 32, 37, & 38.

The guru tells him to meditate on the bull, eat the meals provided for him, and after fifty days, the guru will call him out of the room. The farmer agrees and all arrangements are made.

After fifty days, the door is opened and the guru tells his disciple to come out. But the farmer replies, "No, no. I cannot come through that small opening."

"Why?" asks the guru.

"I am so big, and my horns will not fit through the door."

"Where are your horns?" the guru asks.

"On my head," the farmer answers.

"Who are you?" asks the guru.

"I am a bull."

"Ah, you did very well, my boy," the guru says as he enters the room to push the farmer through the door. When the farmer comes outside, he falls on the ground and goes into *samadhi*. His mind had been trained with a one-pointed focus, making it easy for the guru to shift his focus onto supreme truth.

I recommend a practice from the *Taittirīya Upanishad* with the focus on breath, thought and sound. Breath is very precious to all of us. Our lives are dependent on breath. We constantly receive and release breath; this activity is called *prāna* and *apāna*. *Prāna* is at the root of our senses. Our senses are not active without *prāna*, the life energy that enlivens them. In many scriptures, the senses are even given the name of *prāna*. When we moderate the flow of our *prāna*, we moderate our senses. When we rein in the outward movement of the senses, we purify the mind and make it stable. Mind is nothing but the movement of thoughts. As we moderate the outward movement, we intone an inward thought process – a mantra – that leads to the source of life. Gradually, breath, thought and sound lead us to their source in supreme consciousness.

When we realize the source of our life, we experience pure love, which is oneness, unity. It is impossible to experience pure eternal love with objects that constantly change. Supreme spirit is unchangeable: the eternal abode of blissfulness. When we experience unity with our source, devotion fills our hearts and minds. This liberates us from the motivations of desire and enables us to perform our duties inspired by spirit.

Karma is the motive behind our actions. In our philosophy, there are three parts of action. The action itself is called *kriya*; the doer is called *karta*; and the motive is called *karma*. When our motives are related with devotion to divinity, we do not create bondage or suffering in our lives. Pure love is an infinite ocean. When we experience this abundance, we act from a place of wholeness, and we are able to serve without lust, temptation, or greed.

One great seer declared, "Desire is like a dense darkness, but love is the sunshine of the illuminated self." Pure love eliminates the darkness of desire and inspires us to do what is beneficial for all beings. The seeker who is engaged in the welfare of all beings is a great devotee. "This person is doubtless, controls the mind and senses, is a vessel of divine love engaging in the welfare of all beings, and is perpetually released."[73]

---

[73] *Bhagavad Gītā* V/25.

This is the main idea behind *karma yoga*. If we devote our love to the source of light then we are *yogis*. But if we misuse our love, attaching to the external world, we enter in to an endless cycle of birth and death, clinging and loss. Objects are changeable. They come and go. We suffer because we desire and attach to objects that are part of this cycle. When the objects we enjoy change form, we feel loss and we suffer. The way to end our suffering is available in every moment. Supreme spirit is infinite, eternal, and always the same. We will never feel loss when we attach to divinity.

July 29, 1997
The Enemy is Desire

The result of an action depends on the motive behind the action. Two people in different times, places and circumstances can perform the exact same act and receive totally different results.

A surgeon uses a knife to cut a patient's body and remove disease. The motive behind this action is to help, not harm the person. A thief or rapist, driven by greed, rage or lust, uses a knife to cut into a victim's body. One is considered a helpful member of society and the other a criminal. The different motives behind the same action bring very different results.

A soldier fighting to protect a border kills many invaders and is considered a hero in the eyes of fellow warriors, citizens, and the government. If the same person returns home, quarrels and becomes angry with a neighbor for violating property lines, this person may use a gun to threaten or kill the neighbor. Now the same people who awarded the soldier's bravery would want this person in jail. The actions are similar, but the motives for the actions are different and give different results.

We can worship God, believe in God, and offer our life to God, but we cannot be God. We do not have any control over the way things turn out. But we do have a fundamental choice about the direction of our lives. We can choose to develop demonic tendencies or to nurture divine qualities. There are many stories of demonic people who gained power through extreme measures and then used that power with selfish motives, harming many people. Although powerful, they were selfish and destructive.

Demonic tendencies cannot co-exist with divine qualities. If our motive is to help and serve divinity, then we are divine and it does not matter what actions we perform related with our skills and abilities. Our reason for action and the motivation behind our action is far more meaningful than the action itself. All action is part of *rajoguna*, but our mind may be dominated by *sattoguna*, *rajoguna*, or *tamoguna* as we perform the action. *Sattoguna* is pure, illuminating, and knowledgeful. When *rajoguna* prevails, we experience many emotions, such as desire, lust, passion, greed, anger, pride or temptation. If *tamoguna* is dominant, we are dull, destructive and deluded; we want to be taken care of by others without performing any work.

When a passionate person is unable to fulfill desire, he or she becomes angry. If the passion is satisfied, then greed and temptation are strengthened. Increased desire always follows fulfillment. Desire is the projection of *rajoguna* and it is insatiable. Anger and greed are fueled by unmet desires. As anger increases it becomes more harmful. It first appears as annoyance, then grows from jealousy, to dislike or hatred, and finally emerges as rage. Unless this chain is broken it leads to violence.

Anger is not the root cause of destruction. It grows from unfulfilled desire, and desire is rooted in *rajoguna*. "Passion and anger are both the result of *rajoguna* and are great devourers. They are the enemy of humankind."[74]

---

[74] *Bhagavad Gītā* III/37.

They are insatiable. Fuel on a fire increases the flame, and there is no end to fire's ability to burn the fuel. In the same way, our attempts to fulfill desire only increase our passion and anger. If we fulfill our desire, we want more, and if we fail, we become angry. Desire is voracious, and whether we satisfy it or not, it leads to endless suffering.

Desire is our real enemy, not the people and objects we covet. Desire, and by extension lust, passion, greed, and anger; cause our bondage and misery. Our enemies are created by desire and the emotions engendered by desire. When we talk or behave harshly, we create enmity. When we lie, cheat, mislead, or steal, we create enemies. Manipulating and using others for our own benefit causes conflict. When our behavior is driven by the root cause of desire, we make enemies. We can turn our enemies into friends by establishing helpful motives and engaging in useful behavior. Our behavior creates friends when we are inspired by divinity and foes when we are motivated by desire. We make friends when we devote our abilities, skills, and resources to helping others. When we behave selfishly, we do the opposite; taking and using others' skills, abilities, and assets for our own benefit.

Our life energy projects as emotion. When our emotions are under the control of our intellect and guided by knowledge, we thrive. When our passion is steered by compassion and thoughtfulness, it becomes divine love. But if our passion is under the sway of ignorance and infatuation, it is demonic attachment.

Delusion and infatuation cause demonic action. Our minds are inhabited by the qualities we invite into them. Ruminating on worldly attachments causes lust, greed, and anger to dwell in our minds. Our suffering or happiness is rooted in our thoughts. When our love turns into desire, we push divinity – our source of blissfulness – out of mind.

But the mind can be cleared so that knowledge can be received; we can change our harmful habits and connect with divinity. Divinity resides in every person. Where desire is controlled, there is no pride, anger, or violence. By controlling our desires, we can channel the energy of desire into the power of love.

Life energy is a pure source of love. We have the choice: we can spill our life energy into emotion, or we can direct it toward divinity. If our attachment is with divinity, then we are devotees on the path to lasting happiness. Devotion is possible when we moderate our emotion.

We are carried away by our emotional attachments, but we are uplifted by our attachment to divinity. Krishna tells, "The aspirant who fixes his or her mind on me becomes a *yogi*."[75] When we relate our minds with divinity or a divinely inspired person, our minds take on the qualities of divinity. By thinking upon divinity, divine qualities enliven our thoughts. This is the blessing of grace: the inspirational qualities we dwell on enter our minds.

As we purify our hearts and minds, knowledge and light increase in our intellects. When we are stable in a state of pure knowledge, we are one with divinity. This experience is called *dharma megha samadhi*. Patanjali compares this state to clouds that always shower rain.[76] When we live in this stability, our lives shower virtue and

---

[75]*Bhagavad Gītā* VII/1.
[76] *Yoga Sūtras* 4/29.

we embody tranquility and righteousness. Transforming our emotions into devotion leads us to blissful divinity.

July 30, 1998
Love Seeks Its Source

We are always connected with our divine source. As light is the manifestation of electricity in a light bulb, our life is the manifestation of divine light in our intellect. According to *Sāmkhya* philosophy, light first manifests in our intellect and is followed by further projections of nature into human form. Light appears in the medium of the intellect as consciousness. This awakens our awareness of existence called I-amness or ego. I-amness expresses in the form of love in our heart.[77] The three qualities of supreme spirit – intelligence, existence, and bliss – enliven each medium with light, life, and love. All three qualities are manifestations of our intimate and inseparable source: one supreme consciousness. Our lives are the manifestation of ultimate truth. But when infinity appears in the limited medium of the intellect and projects I-amness, we experience the limitation related with our individual medium. Unfortunately, we accept this limited form as the cause of life, and we believe the individual quality of the medium is the finite quality of life. This leaves us feeling separate and empty.

---

[77] Philosophically, heart is indicated by the word *hridhayam*. *Hri* means inhaling and *dha* means exhaling. *Yam* means this breath. The center that initiates breath is the *brahma chakra*. This point is the true abode of Godhead where supreme consciousness resides.

These feelings create a demand within us to perfect and fulfill ourselves. If we turn this inner demand outwards, it becomes desire. Desire is fueled when we think we can complete ourselves by possessing people or objects outside of ourselves. This mistaken thinking is the root cause of endless cycles of birth and death. Because we turn outward to satisfy ourselves, we have been striving for many lives. Regardless of our effort, we are unable to fulfill our inner demand and achieve happiness.

Desire grows out of our feelings of limitation. When the need to experience perfection is focused externally, it causes our attachment to people and objects. When we realize absolute truth and our position as the manifestation of divine light, we fully comprehend the futility of seeking externally, and turn inside to fulfill our inner demand for wholeness.

A small flame of fire has the same properties of light and heat as a large blaze of fire. Both have the exact same qualities, only the quantity is different. Likewise, we have the same qualities as supreme consciousness. The pure form of our I-amness holds intelligence, existence, and bliss. These qualities are indivisible. When we experience the purity of these qualities within us, we rise above feelings of emptiness and fulfill our inner demand for perfection and wholeness. We shift away from chasing things outside of ourselves and we move toward the source of abundance within. When our attraction to external people and things, which is a form of love, turns inward, it becomes devotion. Devotion leads us to our source of life. This is the essence of the mystical teachings in the *Bhagavad Gītā*, *Vedas*, and *Upanishads*.

When we are grasping in the material world, our love becomes desire and appears in the form of emotion. Desire is endless. It is never satiated; no matter how much we have in our possession, we will always want more. Our feeling of lack will never be made whole by accumulating objects and relationships. No matter how much we hoard, our relationships and possessions are transient and limited, and their instability fuels our desire for more. This downward spiral of desire fueling desire is caused by ignorance.[78] There is only one way for our love to be fulfilled: we must realize that our true self is one with the source of our life.

Desire is not satisfied by accumulation, but it can be removed. When we understand the inner demand of our soul, then we can seek our source, fulfill our inner demand, and end our desire. I-amness works through the mind. The mind engages with people and things through the senses and presents thoughts about the world to our I-amness. Our impressions about the qualities and properties of people and things appear as thoughts. The senses and the mind are attracted by countless externals: people, situations and things. These externals come in endless varieties. No matter how much contact the mind and senses have, desire continues to grow. Desire is voracious.

Dedicated practice is the antidote to desire. We control and moderate our desires and seek to understand the true quality of love. When we allow our expression of love to be directed outwards for consumption and accumulation, we are never satisfied. When we turn our

---

[78] Philosophically, ignorance is the misunderstanding of our true nature.

love toward our divine source, we realize our unity with ultimate truth and we feel whole; there is nothing to desire but this. We are one with infinity, with Godhead. *Karma yoga* directs us to focus on divinity, work according to our abilities and skills, and be content with the remnants of our actions. These remnants are the blessing of divine grace.

We need to realize our proper path and the reason for our journey. What is it that we are truly seeking, and what will satisfy our deepest need? The thirst of desire can never be quenched, but our inner demand for wholeness and perfection is our birthright and can be fulfilled. When we bring our mind under control, think upon the source of our life, and realize our unity with this source, we achieve abundant life energy and love. In time, our love moves beyond the limits of all objects and relationships, and our feelings of limitation and emptiness dissipate.

When we feel separation and lack, we crave and chase; but when we realize the source of life, all experience is full of glory. If we run to catch our shadow, we will never succeed, but if we walk towards the sun, our shadow will follow wherever we go. Swami Ram Tirth tells that when he was interested in the world, the world ran from him. When he turned his eyes away from the world, the world came begging for him to enjoy. When we willingly release our grasping, we prosper. This is the greatness of detachment.

Love is the root of our relations with people and objects; and our life, our I-amness, is the root cause of all variations of love. Both life and love are the effect of one supreme light, the source of our existence. As a ray of light from the sun is never separate from the sun, our life and love are never separate from supreme light. "Supreme light is undivided, but appears divided in all beings. This is to be known as the sustainer of all. It is the light of all lights. It enlightens all of nature and resides in the heart of all. It is this knowledge that is to be attained."[79] Through knowledge, we are able to know and enter into this light. Our supreme source is the goal of all knowledge.

Divine light resides in every *brahma chakra*. It is always within us. We are the manifestation of divine light. To experience this eternal and infinite source of blissfulness, we must devote our life and love to this divine light. Love knows its source. When we turn the attractive power of love within, we realize one supreme light and experience unity and wholeness.

---

[79] *Bhagavad Gītā* XIII/16 & 17.

August 30 & 31, 1995
Yagya

We should not think of ourselves as sinners or that our life energy is polluted. Sin and pollution cannot touch our soul; the soul is part and parcel of divinity, and no power can pollute divinity. As humans, we may be ignorant or engage in harmful behavior, but we are able to change our destructive tendencies into saintly qualities. Krishna tells us, "Even if a sinner worships me with devotion, he or she is thought of as a saint; for once this person turns away from sin he or she is sinless."[80] The self indwelling all beings is pure, regardless of our behavior.

Harmful behavior is the result of wrong impressions stored in the *chitta*. These impressions are patterns of thinking and behaving, which create suffering for our selves and others. Our wrong impressions lead us away from Godhead. Life is the manifestation of pure, supreme light. Within an electric bulb, light is the manifestation of pure electricity. In a clear bulb, the light appears in its full brilliance. But if the bulb is colored, the light appears colored. A red bulb gives off red light, and a blue bulb sheds blue light. The light is pure white brilliance, but the light appears to be the color of the bulb's stained glass.

Supreme spirit is pure. In a pure *chitta*, life appears in pure form: brilliant illuminating intelligence, existence, and bliss. But when our *chitta* is polluted with wrong impressions, then our life appears stained by these

---

[80] *Bhagavad Gītā* IX/30.

impressions. Pollution is generated by the wrong impressions held in our *chitta*, while spirit remains pristine. *Chitta* is essentially a pure medium. In *Sāmkhya* philosophy it is called the intellect, the most subtle projection of nature. It is like a clear crystal, which takes on the color of any object placed near it.

Impurity begins when our soul accepts the chitta and the modifications of this medium as its true form. When the *chitta*, or intellect, is enlivened by spirit, a process of modification begins. This process activates the ego, mind, and senses, enabling them to relate and identify with the external world. This engagement brings the qualities and properties of external experience into the *chitta*. We shape our idea of self by the value we place upon these qualities. The more our definition of self depends on the external world, the more pollution we collect in our *chitta*. Our false identification colors our *chitta*. Wrong impressions are held in the *chitta* because we identify with and attach to the qualities of nature. I-amness is not polluted because it is above nature, and is the observer of nature.

The spiritual path advises the detachment of the observer. We need to be alert to the value we place on anything or anyone external to our true self. We must become aware of the ways we mistakenly use external factors to define ourselves. It is possible to live with purity in the world; we can perform service, using worldly objects to maintain, sustain, and develop our bodies, minds, and intellects. To do this, we must wake up and recognize the value we place on objects, and learn to appreciate the true self. When we hold external qualities above the self, our ignorance causes suffering. By shifting our perspective and realizing the ultimate value of our real self, we learn how to perform our duty while remaining free from the limiting effects of nature.

We have chosen all of the beliefs and impressions we hold. And we can choose to let go of any impression that does not uplift our spiritual development. We can release our limiting attachments and our finite idea of self. It is possible for us to learn how to live among nature and act in nature, while attached to divinity and aligned with infinity.

We would not survive a single moment without the activity of nature. Our intellect, ego, mind, five cognitive senses, five active senses, and the five primordial elements of the gross body are always with us. We cannot take our body anywhere without interacting with the primordial elements. We are always in space; we need air for life energy; we require heat inside to maintain a healthy temperature; and we thrive with water and food. All five elements are necessary for survival. In my days of intense practice, I left my home with one change of clothing and begged for a small amount of food once daily. I lived in remote places, away from the company of others. I climbed eighteen thousand feet to the top of a mountain in the Himalayas. While meditating there, I realized that the five primordial elements were still with me. Food was the source of my body; heat and water were present in my body; and I was breathing oxygen into the space of my lungs. There was no place where I could be free from nature.

Nature includes the subtle body. Even when we leave our physical bodies and are free of the gross primordial elements, the subtle body remains. This subtle body consists of the subtle elements of nature,[81] mind and ego. Even the causal body, our *chitta*, is a projection of nature. We cannot exist free from nature. Nature is the divine power of Godhead that allows this universe to manifest. Nature is nature. We cannot leave nature, but we can understand and detach from the qualities of nature and attach to the qualities of supreme light.

Supreme light resides in our *brahma chakra* as our true self, our soul. According to the *Taittirīya Upanishad*, our individual soul functions through five levels: the sheaths of intellect, ego, mind, senses, and body. When consciousness is active at any of these levels, it assumes the parameters of that sheath. Thus we have intelligence consciousness; ego consciousness, which is our awareness of I-amness; mind consciousness or thought; awareness associated with the activity of the senses; and physical awareness or identification with the body.

In *Sāmkhya*, these sheaths are projections and transformations of energy. Consciousness is active within the different forms of energy, but this does not limit consciousness. The purpose of *yoga* practice and meditation is to understand that consciousness is separate from the limitations of energy. Consciousness has its own properties of existence, intelligence, and bliss. It is unfettered and unaffected by the limitations of the instruments through which it functions.

There is a unique sacrificial process for each sheath. Krishna names these five forms of sacrifice or *yagya*: *dravya*

---

[81] The subtle elements of nature are the five *tanmatras* of sound, touch, sight, taste and smell. According to *Sāmkhya* philosophy, these subtle elements project the five gross elements: the *bhutas* of space, air, fire, water and earth.

for the body, *tapah* for the senses, *yoga* for the mind, *svadhyaya* for the ego, and *jnana* for the intellect.[82] We sacrifice when we offer what we have for the welfare of all beings and for the whole projection of divinity. When we do this, we transform our humanity into divinity.

Dravya yagya is related with the physical world of the five primordial elements. At this level, we perform our duties related with our abilities and skills. We work on behalf of divinity manifesting in all names and forms. Everything we see is a projection of divine power. And everything we do should be an offering to Godhead. Although we are mindful to sustain ourselves, we do not work for wealth and accumulation.

It is important to understand that everything we receive, use and share comes from the same divine elements and is a projection of divine power. Natural resources are for all beings, not only human beings. Living things all share life energy from the same infinite source. When we perceive this, we are able to realize the underlying unity in this diverse world. One enlivening power inhabits many different names and forms. We are part of this unity and we should devote ourselves and our resources to this divine power. Once we realize our oneness with all, we see the absurdity of selfish actions, such as hoarding wealth or consuming more than we need. We should try to help and feed others, and not accumulate beyond what is truly useful to us. Living with an understanding of oneness, we are motivated to care for others, and we lose the desire to accumulate beyond our

---

[82] *Bhagavad Gītā* IV/28.

needs. We choose to live simply with respect for the divine elements and this divine projection.

Special attention should be given to those who have exceptional challenges in their lives, such as people with disabilities or students with limited means. These people are vessels of our compassion. And yet, we must use our discrimination when giving and sacrificing; laziness is sometimes the cause of misfortune and this form of *tamoguna* should not be rewarded.

Tapah yagya is the form of sacrifice at the level of the senses. *Tapah* is austerity, and restraint is needed for bringing our senses under control. We can meet our needs, but we will never satisfy our desire. Desire is limitless and voracious. Our senses must be moderated in order to rein in our cravings. The process of moderating, controlling, and checking our senses is *tapah yagya*.

Our cognitive and active senses play an important role. The cognitive senses collect information from the environment and report this information to our higher faculties. We use our active senses to maintain and sustain our physical bodies, interact with others, create progeny, and foster mental balance and acuity. The senses have many roles beyond satisfying the cravings of the mind. At the level of the senses, we refrain from stimulating desire. We discipline our senses and develop their use as tools for service.

The third form of sacrifice is related with the mind. *Yoga yagya* is meditation. Our mind functions in the middle of the five sheaths of consciousness. If we allow our minds to follow the body and senses, we degrade ourselves and are unable to fulfill our inner demand for wholeness. We train our minds and turn towards divinity.

The mind is a projection of ego. Mind is simply waves of thought: our I-amness engaging with the physical and subtle world. *Yoga* turns our minds towards our cause, bringing our minds under the control of ego and intellect. Allowing the mind to wander with the senses and the body is *bhoga*, not *yoga*. Through *bhoga*, we may temporarily enjoy and glimpse happiness, but ultimately we suffer. To find lasting happiness, we devote our minds and emotions to the divine path. We withdraw our thoughts from outside and fix our thinking on infinity. Gradually, divine thoughts pervade our minds and we become doubtless, lustless, and desireless.

The mind can drag us down or lift us up. Bondage and freedom are related with our thoughts. When the mind is attached with the objects of the senses, we are bound, but when the mind detaches, we experience freedom. In meditation, we focus on infinity. By thinking upon infinity in the form of endless space, we release our mental bondage and remove ideas of limitation. It is also helpful to visualize our breath coming and going from the infinite source of life energy shared by all beings.

All limitations and barriers are created in our minds, and we must work hard to remove them. No power, no guru, not even infinite Godhead can remove our limitations for us if we are not determined to be free of them. But when we are inspired to remove our obstacles and limitations, divine power supports our efforts in many ways.

At the level of ego, we need *svadhyaya*, self-study. Ego is the manifestation of individuation. We are aware of our existence because of ego. *Svadhyaya yagya* is self-introspection. We focus our attention inside and work to understand the qualities and behaviors of our true self. How does our ego work and act? What are its aims and motives? Beyond this, we seek the meaning and cause of I-amness. Where does our sense of existence originate? This practice leads us to the source of our individual I-amness, the source of all life.

Our I-amness emerges from spirit and nature. When spirit manifests in the medium of the *chitta* or intellect, this initial movement of nature stimulates awareness in the form of a pure sense of existence called I-amness. Spirit is infinite consciousness and knowledge, and nature is infinite power and energy. Both are eternal and infinite, but spirit is imperishable and unchangeable, while nature is perishable and changes in every moment.

Nature is the source of all forms including the body, senses, mind, ego, and intellect. Our soul is the manifestation of supreme spirit, and ego is the agent of supreme spirit in nature. When we understand this unfoldment of nature and devote our I-amness to Godhead, we come to realize our ego has no separate existence from Godhead. Ego is Godhead engaging with this universe. Patanjali explains, "Even though these instruments have fulfilled their purpose for that seer who has attained realization and perfection, these instruments are not finished because they are universal for all others."[83] When we attain realization, our *chitta* and its modifications of intellect, ego, and mind continue to serve divinity. They are not destroyed, but are devoted to supreme consciousness. This devotion is our sacrifice.

---

[83] *Yoga Sūtras* II/22.

Jnana yagya is the process of discriminating between the qualities of spirit and the properties of nature. We use our intellect to discern that spirit and nature work together to project our individual existence. We realize that their coming together, which is called *sanyoga*, enables us to perceive the separate qualities and distinct powers of spirit and nature.[84] Without this understanding, we believe spirit and nature are one power and we attribute the qualities of spirit to the medium of nature. This is *avidya* or ignorance.[85] When we remove this misunderstanding, our suffering ends and our soul is liberated.[86]

"True knowledge is knowing spirit and nature distinctly."[87] "When a person achieves this knowledge he achieves identity with Godhood."[88] This is the aim of life. Our behavior is nothing but a projection of our ideas, and our ideas are the projection of the impressions we have etched into the intellect. Knowledge is at the root of our lives and is the basis for our actions and our faith. True faith evolves from what we know to be true; knowledge does not grow out of our beliefs. If we do not seek knowledge as the basis of our understanding, we become more and more entrenched in the quirks of our misunderstanding. Individual personality is the expression of impressions held in the intellect. Krishna explains, "Humans are made of faith, whatever people believe, thus they are."[89]

---

[84] *Yoga Sūtras* II/23.
[85] *Yoga Sūtras* II/24.
[86] *Yoga Sūtras* II/25.
[87] *Bhagavad Gītā* XIII/2.
[88] *Bhagavad Gītā* XIV/2.
[89] *Bhagavad Gītā* XVII/3.

Knowledge lifts us higher, while ignorance and desire cause our downfall. Intellect is the highest and most developed instrument of our body. The intellect holds the capacity for discrimination and wisdom. It is the abode of pure knowledge and the root of our individual life.

In the *Upanishads*, our intellect is considered the charioteer and the body is the chariot. Our soul is the rider of the chariot. As the intellect is the charioteer, the mind is the reins. The senses are the horses, and the material world is the attractive grassy land along the path. The wise say that the individual soul is the passenger, involved with the ego, mind, and senses and enjoying the ride.[90] When we lack wisdom and have a distracted mind, our senses are as uncontrollable as wild and vicious horses, unable to take the chariot ahead. But when we develop wisdom and a steady mind, our senses are controlled like the well-trained horses of a skilled charioteer.[91] We cannot achieve the supreme experience if, without insight or discrimination, we have an undisciplined mind and live an impure life. Without steady practice, we move in the cycle of birth and death. But when we work to become conscious and wise, living with purity and discipline, we are on the path to attain that highest good, never returning to take birth in this mortal world. A wise charioteer keeps control of the reins of the mind, completes the journey, and reaches the destination of the highest place where supreme *Brahman* resides.[92]

We are not the slave of our senses. We are the master of our senses. It is our weakness and ignorance that cause

---

[90] *Katha Upanishad* 1.3.3 & 4.
[91] *Katha Upanishad* 1.3.5 & 6.
[92] *Katha Upanishad* 1.3.7-9.

us to be bound by desires. "Our senses are greater than the objects of senses. Our mind is higher than the senses. And beyond our mind is our intellect, which is the abode of pure consciousness and knowledge.[93] Our intellect is the master of this body. We need to turn our intellect towards the source of life. Turning the intellect means turning the eye of wisdom towards its source.

The sacrifice of knowledge has three parts. We turn, we hold, and we offer. We put our intellect into divinity and receive divine power and qualities; we hold and preserve this knowledge and power; and we offer this to others. The highest level of *yagya* is turning our intellect towards divinity, and encouraging others along this path. When we do this, our minds become filled with divine love and mercy. Compassion fills our hearts, and we devote our lives to uplifting others, so that they may enjoy the same divine experience.

We need steadfast practice to accomplish this higher state. A potter's work is only finished when the pot is fired. After throwing the pot on a wheel and skillfully shaping the clay, firing makes the pot a solid container for water. Our bodies, minds, and intellects are like pots. If we increase divine energy in our lives without first disciplining ourselves and increasing virtue, we will not be able to hold divine energy. It will quickly dissipate. All *yoga* practices, especially breathing exercises, are a kind of fire that makes our bodies, minds, and intellects pure and stable. Breath, *prāna*, is our active power, our life energy. Krishna explains, that "Breath is an oblation we offer into the

---

[93] *Bhagavad Gītā* III/42.

divine fire. It is a *yagya*, a vital sacrifice. No one can survive without this essential *yagya*."[94]

Krishna advises, "*Yagya*, *tapah*, and *dana* are not to be abandoned, but rather performed. They are great purifiers of those who are wise."[95] When our soul appears in our *brahma chakra*, two kinds of activity begin. The first activity is *prāna*, the receiving and giving of breath, which is a form of *yagya*. The second activity is *tapah*. In this verse, *tapah* refers to the expression of consciousness, which allows our intellect to become active with awareness and thought. *Prāna* and thought are always present in the light of our real self. The third action Krishna encourages is *dana*, offering or donating to others.

In this verse, all *yagya*, all sacrifice, is related with breath. When the *yagya* of our vital breath ends, our bodies die. Breath is very precious. It is life. Whenever we engage in activity, we expend our life energy. We are only able to engage with objects and relationships because we are alive, and we are alive because we receive breath.

Tapah means austerity, and here Krishna is referring to austerity of thought, putting our minds into divinity, into the light of knowledge. *Yagya* and *tapah* are two processes needed to achieve divinity. Through *yagya*, we achieve physical, sensual, and mental refinement. With *tapah*, we achieve higher knowledge. We should make every effort to increase and hold our life energy, and use our thoughts to analyze truth. First, we receive divine energy and gain strength, ability, and power. Then we discriminate how to use this energy and increase our knowledge. And finally,

---

[94] *Bhagavad Gītā* IV/29.
[95] *Bhagavad Gītā* XVIII/5.

through *dana*, we use our increased knowledge and energy as offerings for the welfare of all beings.

May God bless you all. May He lead you from darkness to light, from unreal to real, from death to immortality. May He shower upon you all His divine grace. May He bestow upon you all His divine love and wisdom. Peace in the heaven. Peace in the space. Peace on the earth.

Bibliography

Audio Lectures:

1. Brahmrishi Vishvatma Bawra. 1995. Lectures on *Bhagavad Gītā*, Fourth Chapter. Kent Ashram, Ohio.
2. Brahmrishi Vishvatma Bawra. 1997. Lectures on *Karma Yoga*. Kent Ashram, Ohio.
3. Brahmrishi Vishvatma Bawra. 1998. Lectures on *Bhagavad Gītā*, Third Chapter. Kent Ashram, Ohio.

Books based on lectures by Brahmrishi Vishvatma Bawra:

1. *Essays on Karma Yoga*. Compiled by William & Margot Milcetich. 2001. Divine Radiance Press.
2. *Nature of Sacrifice*. 2003. Compiled and edited by Margot Milcetich, Divine Radiance Press.

Other Books:

1. Bal Gangadhar Tilak. 1986. *Srimad Bhagavadgītā-Rahasya*, Sixth Edition, Pune, India. Geeta Printers.
2. Winthrop Sargeant. 1994. *The Bhagavad Gītā*, Albany, New York: State University of New York Press.